BAREFOOT CONTESSA
FAMILY STYLE

INA GARTEN

BAREFOOT CONTESSA

FAMILY STYLE

BANTAM PRESS

LONDON · NEW YORK · TORONTO · SYDNEY · AUCKLAND

TRANSWORLD PUBLISHERS
61–63 Uxbridge Road, London W5 5SA
A Random House Group Company
www.transworldbooks.co.uk

First published in the United States by Clarkson Potter/Publishers, New York
member of the Crown Publishing Group
a division of Random House, Inc.

First published in Great Britain
in 2012 by Bantam Press
an imprint of Transworld Publishers

Copyright © Ina Garten, 2002, 2012
Photographic copyright © Maura McEvoy 2002, 2012

Recipe: "Mashed Yellow Turnips with Crispy Shallots"
from *The Union Square Cafe Cookbook* by Danny Meyer and Michael Romano.
Copyright © 1994 by Danny Meyer and Michael Romano.
Reprinted by permission of HarperCollins Publishers, Inc.

Ina Garten has asserted her right under the Copyright, Designs
and Patents Act 1988 to be identified as the author of this work.

A CIP catalogue record for this book
is available from the British Library.

ISBN 9780593068441

Addresses for Random House Group Ltd companies outside the UKcan be found at: www.randomhouse.co.uk
The Random House Group Ltd Reg. No. 954009

Printed and bound in China

2 4 6 8 10 9 7 5 3 1

CONVERSION CHART

Oven Temperatures:	Spoon Measures:	American Solid Measures:	Liquid Measures:
130°C = 250°F = Gas mark ½	1 level tablespoon flour = 15g	1 cup rice US = 225g	1 cup US = 275ml
150°C = 300°F = Gas mark 2	1 heaped tablespoon flour = 28g	1 cup flour US = 115g	1 pint US = 550ml
180°C = 350°F = Gas mark 4	1 level tablespoon sugar = 28g	1 cup butter US = 225g	1 quart US = 900ml
190°C = 375°F = Gas mark 5	1 level tablespoon butter = 15g	1 stick butter US = 115g	
200°C = 400°F = Gas mark 6		1 cup dried fruit US = 225g	
220°C = 425°F = Gas mark 7		1 cup brown sugar US = 180g	
230°C = 450°F = Gas mark 8		1 cup granulated sugar US = 225g	

For Jeffrey,
who makes all my dreams come true

THANKS

So many creative people work on my books. Maura McEvoy, thank you for all the gorgeous photographs; Rori Trovato—again!—knocks my socks off with her food styling, wonderful ideas, and sense of humor; and Miguel Flores-Vianna always brings such style and fun to all of our shoots. I can't imagine writing books without all of you. Also behind the scenes are Pam Krauss, my amazing editor; Marysarah Quinn, the sweetest book designer ever; Barbara Marks, my enthusiastic publicist; the unfailingly supportive Lauren Shakely at Clarkson Potter, Chip Gibson, formerly at Crown; and Esther Newberg at ICM. You all make me feel so special.

Parker Hodges and Amy Baiata Forst of Barefoot Contessa are a constant inspiration for me—thank you for supporting my new career. I couldn't be doing it without you.

And thank you to all my friends and family who show up for photo shoots at all times of the day or night, and most certainly when they have better things to do: my sweet husband Jeffrey Garten, Frank Newbold, Antonia Bellanca Mahoney, Tess Mahoney, Cecily Stranahan, Mike and Taylor Lupica (and family), Johnson and Janice McKelvy (and family), Lock McKelvy, Ken Wright, and Marilyn Bethany. And for Stephen Drucker, who artfully arranges to be out of the country during photo shoots, thank you for your constant support and unerring judgment. Thanks also to Ellen Burnie for her brilliant creative guidance and energy.

Also, thank you to all the fabulous friends who contributed recipes for this book: Eli Zabar from Eli's Bread, Eli's Manhattan, et al.!; George Germon and Johanne Killeen from Al Forno in Providence, Rhode Island; Danny Meyer from Union Square Cafe in New York City; Anna Pump from Loaves and Fishes in Sagaponack, New York; Devon Fredericks and Susan Costner; Brent Newsom from Brent Newsom Caterer of East Hampton, New York; and Laura Donnelly from The Laundry Restaurant in East Hampton, New York.

And most of all, I can't imagine spending my day without my friend and partner in crime, Barbara Libath. Thanks for making *everything* so much fun.

Contents

WELCOME HOME

Over the past three years, I've been lucky enough to be asked to speak to groups all over the country and I've met wonderful people. Each time I try to ask my audience, "What kinds of recipes would you like to have?" The response is always the same: people want more easy recipes that they can make for their families—and for the dear friends they consider close enough to *be* family.

We all know that families now aren't necessarily like Ozzie and Harriet. (It turns out even Ozzie and Harriet's family wasn't all "Ozzie and Harriet"!) Family has a traditional context, but today it's not as simple as two parents with 2.3 kids. It's about relationships. It's about people who are bound together by love and a sense of being responsible for one another. It's spouses with no children, like Jeffrey and me; it's a group of women who meet to cook dinner together once a month; it's a one-parent family with adopted children; and it's two men who've made a life together. AT THE END OF THE DAY, ALL WE HAVE IS LOVE. GETTING LOVE, BUT EVEN MORE, *FEELING* LOVE. It's those feelings that let me know all the suffering in the world can be healed if we just stick together. And our families, no matter how we define them, are the glue.

This idea of family is behind much of what defines my cooking style. I want everyone who comes to my house to feel like family. I'll share with you lots of the ways I do this when I entertain, setting the stage (or the table) for sharing, connecting, and creating a true sense of community. People who have had this experience with you will go home feeling nurtured and loved, and the good news is, so will you.

Setting the Table

I really like to entertain in the kitchen. I think it's cozier and more personal than the dining room. The roast is coming out of the oven, dessert is on the counter, the dishes are in the sink; and it has an energy that I love. And best of all, I never have to leave the party to serve the next course. As I've said many times, a round table seems to me to create the best setting for people to really connect; no one is left out of the conversation down at the end. I always have low candles, which represent the traditional fire in the hearth, and low flowers or decorations that don't impede anyone's view. Bottles of water and wine are set out for everyone to help themselves—and each other. DINNER MIGHT BE SOMETHING SERVED FROM A BIG PLATTER IN THE MIDDLE OF THE TABLE.

A few summers ago, I gave a charity dinner at my house. Inevitably, most people at this kind of event don't know one another, so how was I going to help them make that initial contact? While I obviously couldn't have thirty-two people for dinner in my kitchen, I still wanted the guests to feel warm and connected. I decided to set up four small round tables of eight in the dining room, all very cozy. We served a simple tomato, mozzarella, and basil salad to start and then put huge steaming bowls filled with our Kitchen Clambake from my first cookbook in the middle of each table. Everyone rolled up their sleeves and dove in with their hands. People were passing lobsters and corn, everyone got into the fun, and I was delighted to see that all the tables had very lively discussions.

Cooking Together

Most people wouldn't bat an eye about asking their sister to help with dinner, so why are we so reluctant to ask the friends we invite to our house? WOULDN'T YOU BE FLATTERED IF A FRIEND SAID "I'D LOVE IT!" WHEN YOU OFFERED TO HELP? I'd feel valued and part of the A team. When my friends come for dinner, often I serve the main course, but I'll ask someone else to pour wine, and a third person to help me with dessert, so we're all in it together. It's a community, it's collaborative, and it's so much more fun (not to mention easier!). I have to admit, I've never relaxed to the point that I can let people help

me with the dishes, but if you are comfortable with that, hey, why not?

My friend and assistant Barbara Libath actually took this collaborative idea to her daughter Rebecca's wedding. Here's another case where groups of people often won't know one another and it's a great challenge to get them connected quickly. Rebecca requested that each table of ten people sing a song about love at some point during the wedding dinner. Over the course of the afternoon, one group or another would get up and sing something like the Beatles' "All You Need Is Love" or Elvis's "Love Me Tender." It was funny, it was charming, and everyone had a fabulous time.

Traditions

Every family has traditions—events that they repeat year after year. These traditions give us all a sense of place and community. Most Americans celebrate the Fourth of July and Thanksgiving every year, but there are so many other traditions worth creating. I share lots of observances with friends, from the silly ones like the Academy Awards dinner at my house, to birthdays, New Year's Eve, and our treasured Christmases with the Newbolds. TRADITIONS REASSURE US THAT WE BELONG TOGETHER, AND FOR ME, THAT'S SO GROUNDING. I love them all.

My friend Cecily Stranahan's family has a truly wonderful tradition that I highly recommend to everyone. Each holiday, all thirteen of them (and growing!) cook the entire meal together. The good cooks prepare the main course, the new cooks make the salad (one confirmed non-cook always makes the raisin and nut mix for snacking!), and everyone else is assigned to the cleanup crew. They have a great time, no one is saddled with the entire responsibility for making dinner, and the tradition reaffirms their sense of community.

I hope you'll find lots of ideas and recipes in this book that will make even your friends feel like family. I'd like to think that when I invite friends to my house, they know what I'm *really* saying is, "I love you; come for dinner."

PLANNING THE MEAL

One thing I learned from more than twenty years of catering is that the most relaxed parties are the ones that are well planned. When everything from the menu to the music has been thought out ahead of time, there's nothing left for me to do on the day of the event besides sit back and have fun.

Planning a meal is a lot like solving a jigsaw puzzle. There are lots of things to consider: What's the tone of the party—is it fancy or casual? Is it a sit-down dinner or a buffet with plates on your lap (not my favorite, but sometimes there's no choice)? How much time (and oven space!) do I have? And last but not least, what do *I* want to make? I start by writing down things my guests love to eat: Do they hate fish and crave rice pudding? Nothing says "I love you" to friends more clearly than making their favorite foods.

Of course even the best-laid plans can be thrown off course by late arrivals, special requests, even genuine disasters (of both the natural and man-made varieties). Over the years I've developed strategies for coping with them all—as well as the perspective to realize that if I'm with people I truly care about, the evening is already a success and the rest is just details.

Making a Schedule

It's the day of the party. You've planned the menu and done the shopping. And now you're looking at all the things you have to cook. What were you thinking? It's not possible to make six things between now and 11 A.M. when the guests are due to arrive for brunch! We've all been there.

FOR EVERY PARTY I GIVE, I MAKE A TIMETABLE. I don't mean something scribbled on a paper napkin. I mean a real schedule of what has to happen and when—10:00: turn on the oven; 10:15: turn on the second oven; 10:30: bake the blueberry muffins; 10:35: bake the frittata; 11:00: make the coffee; 11:15: toast the bagels.

When I'm making a schedule, I work backwards. If guests are arriving at

11:00 A.M. and I want to serve breakfast at 11:30, then the frittata has to come out of the oven at 11:25. Since it bakes for 50 minutes, I know it has to go into the oven at 10:35 and the oven has to go on at 10:15. Next, I'll figure out the blueberry muffins: I want them warm, but not hot, so they need to go into the oven at 10:30, come out at 11:00, and then sit on a baking rack to cool for 30 minutes. For dessert, the fruit and honey vanilla yogurt can be made a day ahead and stored in the refrigerator until it's time to serve them.

Planning like this works for two reasons—first, I don't spend the morning endlessly reminding myself when I have to start the final cooking—I just look at my schedule. And second, before I do the shopping, I know for sure I can actually *do* the menu—I haven't chosen three things that cook at different temperatures when I have only one oven available, for example. How many times have you done that?

A little planning goes a long way toward avoiding disaster. A simple schedule can bring you confidence that your party will be really fun.

Finicky Eaters

There's one at every party. Someone who's on a diet. A vegetarian. A friend who's allergic to mustard. And then there are the guests who are just plain difficult. However, most people with food problems aren't trying to be difficult. When confronted with a special request, this is what I do. First, I REMIND MYSELF THAT THESE ARE MY *FRIENDS.* Since I try to invite only people I love, I want them to be happy; instead of being annoyed, I see it as a challenge. Second, instead of planning what I want to serve and then making something extra for the finicky eater, I plan the meal around their needs so they don't feel that they're putting me out. For example, if I know someone is allergic to nuts, I just bake the apple crisp I'd planned for dessert without the walnuts in the topping. Finally, I bear in mind that everyone doesn't have to eat everything. I often make several dishes so people can choose what they want to eat. Planning on making a Sunday rib roast for Christmas? Make a substantial dish like Sagaponack

corn pudding plus sautéed carrots and string beans with shallots to go with it. A vegetarian guest will have a delicious and satisfying meal without the roast and not feel that she's being a problem.

It takes a little extra thought, but each of your guests will feel that you cared enough to do something special for them—and isn't that really what entertaining is all about?

When Disaster Strikes

Several years ago, a friend of mine decided to impress her new husband by making him Thanksgiving dinner. She prepared the turkey, put it in the oven, and said, "Let's take a walk while the turkey cooks." When she came back to baste the turkey an hour later she found that she couldn't open the oven door; apparently, instead of setting the oven on "bake," she had set it on "clean"! "Patti! What did you do?" I asked her. "Well," she replied, "I served the turkey with lots of gravy. It was *very* clean!"

We all have disasters and of course they only seem to happen at the worst possible times. I've planned to spend the day cooking and then had an emergency at the office. Or I've invited four people for a cozy dinner in the kitchen and they've each called to ask if they could bring their houseguests (a particular favorite of mine!). A friend once gave a dinner party for twenty and as she was leading everyone to their seats, she discovered that the dogs had jumped on the table and eaten all the appetizers.

If something like this happens when you are entertaining, don't panic! IF THE PROBLEM CAN EASILY BE FIXED, THEN CERTAINLY FIX IT. IF IT CAN'T, JUST GET PAST IT! Go into the living room, clap your hands, and say, "Well, the dogs ate the appetizers, so we're going directly to the roast chicken!" Instead of making your friends uncomfortable that you're stressed, go on with the evening. And, if worse truly comes to worst, you can always order Chinese takeout and serve it on your best china with a glass of champagne, and you can all have a good laugh about it for years to come.

Baby Spinach
5.50 1/4 LB

STARTERS

EAST HAMPTON Clam Chowder

Chicken Noodle SOUP

Roasted Vegetable SOUP

BRIOCHE Croutons

Smoked Salmon SPREAD

BUFFALO Chicken Wings

Tuna TARTARE

Arugula WITH PARMESAN

Green Salad WITH
CREAMY MUSTARD VINAIGRETTE

Endive, Stilton & WALNUTS

PARMESAN Roasted Asparagus

EAST HAMPTON CLAM CHOWDER

Serves 6 to 8

This soup is a variation on a recipe from the original Loaves and Fishes Cookbook *written by friends Devon Fredericks and Susan Costner. Instead of the usual bland cream and clams, this one is like a clam stew with lots of vegetables and just a bit of milk to finish. You can make it a day in advance and reheat it slowly before dinner.*

12 tablespoons (1½ sticks) unsalted butter, divided
2 cups chopped yellow onions (2 onions)
2 cups medium-diced celery (4 stalks)
2 cups medium-diced carrots (6 carrots)
4 cups peeled medium-diced boiling potatoes (8 potatoes)
1½ teaspoons minced fresh thyme leaves (½ teaspoon dried)
1 teaspoon kosher salt
½ teaspoon freshly ground black pepper
1 quart (4 cups) clam juice
½ cup all-purpose flour
2 cups milk
3 cups chopped fresh chowder clams (1½ pounds shucked clams)

Melt 4 tablespoons (½ stick) of the butter in a large heavy-bottomed stockpot. Add the onions and cook over medium-low heat for 10 minutes, or until translucent. Add the celery, carrots, potatoes, thyme, salt, and pepper and sauté for 10 more minutes. Add the clam juice, bring to a boil, and simmer, uncovered, until the vegetables are tender, about 20 minutes.

In a small pot, melt the remaining 8 tablespoons of butter and whisk in the flour. Cook over very low heat for 3 minutes, stirring constantly. Whisk in a cup of the hot broth and then pour this mixture back into the cooked vegetables. Simmer for a few minutes until the broth is thickened.

Add the milk and clams and heat gently for a few minutes to cook the clams. Taste for salt and pepper. Serve hot.

If you use bottled clam juice instead of fresh, you may need to add more salt.

CHICKEN NOODLE SOUP

Serves 6

Forget canned soup—this is the real thing. And wouldn't we all feel better after eating a bowl? I love having homemade chicken stock in the freezer so I can make this soup in a hurry.

> 1 whole (2 split) chicken breast, bone in, skin on
> Olive oil
> Kosher salt
> Freshly ground black pepper
> 2 quarts homemade Chicken Stock (page 93)
> 1 cup medium-diced celery (2 stalks)
> 1 cup medium-diced carrots (3 carrots)
> 2 cups wide egg noodles
> ¼ cup chopped fresh parsley

Preheat the oven to 350 degrees.

Place the chicken breast on a sheet pan and rub the skin with olive oil. Sprinkle generously with salt and pepper. Roast for 35 to 40 minutes, until cooked through. When cool enough to handle, remove the meat from the bones, discard the skin, and shred or dice the chicken meat.

Bring the chicken stock to a simmer in a large pot and add the celery, carrots, and noodles. Simmer uncovered for about 10 minutes, until the noodles are cooked. Add the cooked chicken meat and parsley and heat through.

Season to taste and serve.

I use Goodman's wide egg noodles.

ROASTED VEGETABLE SOUP

Serves 6 to 8

I love a recipe that uses leftovers. When I'm making roasted vegetables for dinner, I'll make a double batch and have extras for soup the next day. This is a very versatile recipe—you can also throw in last night's mashed potatoes and even the tossed green salad from lunch! It all adds wonderful flavor and goodness. And how else can you get vegetables into your kids without their knowing it?

6 to 8 cups chicken stock, preferably homemade (page 93)
1 recipe Roasted Winter Vegetables (page 110)
Kosher salt and freshly ground black pepper

FOR SERVING
Brioche Croutons (page 34)
Good olive oil

In a large saucepan, heat 6 cups of chicken stock. In two batches, coarsely puree the roasted vegetables and the chicken stock in the bowl of a food processor fitted with the steel blade. Pour the soup back into the pot and season to taste. Thin with more chicken stock and reheat. The soup should be thick but not like a vegetable puree, so add more chicken stock and/or water until it's the consistency you like.

Serve with brioche croutons and a drizzle of good olive oil.

BRIOCHE CROUTONS

Makes 6 to 8 cups

Aren't the croutons the best part of a Caesar salad? These croutons are made with brioche bread and they're delicious in soup or on a salad. One day I put some out with drinks and they all disappeared! This is a great way to use that leftover bread in the freezer.

1 12-ounce brioche loaf or challah
2 tablespoons good olive oil
½ teaspoon kosher salt
¼ teaspoon freshly ground black pepper

Preheat the oven to 350 degrees.

Slice the bread about ¾ inch thick. Cut off the crusts and then cut the slices in ¾-inch dice. You should have 6 to 8 cups of croutons.

Place the croutons on a sheet pan and toss them with the olive oil, salt, and pepper. Bake for 10 to 15 minutes, tossing once, until they're nicely browned on all sides. Cool to room temperature before using and store in a sealed plastic bag.

SMOKED SALMON SPREAD

We started to make this dip at Barefoot Contessa to use up extra smoked salmon, but it was so popular that we had to buy more salmon just to make it. This is my idea of the perfect "no-cook" appetizer to serve with drinks. And the good news is that it actually tastes better if you make it a few days early.

8 ounces cream cheese, at room temperature
½ cup sour cream
1 tablespoon freshly squeezed lemon juice
1 tablespoon minced fresh dill
1 teaspoon prepared horseradish, drained
½ teaspoon kosher salt
¼ teaspoon freshly ground black pepper
¼ pound (4 ounces) smoked salmon, minced

Cream the cheese in an electric mixer fitted with a paddle attachment until just smooth. Add the sour cream, lemon juice, dill, horseradish, salt, and pepper, and mix. Add the smoked salmon and mix well. Chill and serve with crudités or crackers.

If you can find it, I prefer Norwegian salmon; it's drier and less salty than other smoked salmon.

BUFFALO CHICKEN WINGS

Makes 32 pieces

My assistant Barbara Libath and I know that if we test a recipe during the day and we both go home and make it for dinner, it's a winner. These chicken wings, which are broiled not fried, passed that test. Served with the traditional blue cheese dip and celery sticks, they're delicious!

FOR THE WINGS
16 chicken wings (about 3 pounds)
¼ pound (1 stick) unsalted butter
1 teaspoon cayenne pepper
4 teaspoons Frank's Hot Sauce, or 1 teaspoon Tabasco sauce
1 teaspoon kosher salt

FOR THE DIP
1½ cups crumbled gorgonzola or other blue cheese
1 cup good mayonnaise
¾ cup sour cream
2 tablespoons milk
¾ teaspoon Worcestershire sauce
1½ teaspoons kosher salt
¾ teaspoon freshly ground black pepper

Celery sticks, for serving

Preheat the broiler.

Cut the chicken wings in thirds, cutting between the bones. Discard the wing tips. Melt the butter and add the cayenne, hot sauce, and salt. Put the wings on a sheet pan and brush them with the melted butter. Broil them about 3 inches below the heat for 8 minutes. Turn the wings, brush them again with the butter, and broil for 4 more minutes, or until cooked.

For the dip, place the blue cheese, mayonnaise, sour cream, milk, Worcestershire, salt, and pepper in the bowl of a food processor fitted with a steel blade. Process until almost smooth.

Serve the chicken wings hot or at room temperature with the blue cheese dip and celery sticks.

TUNA TARTARE

Serves 6 to 8

On one of my book tours, Barbara Libath and I found ourselves at the fabulous Regent Beverly Wilshire Hotel in Los Angeles. After we stopped running around the rooms exclaiming, "There are two bathrooms! There are four televisions!" we went to the bar downstairs to meet some friends. We were served a fresh tuna tartare that I had to come home and try to re-create. I think this is close.

3/4 pound very fresh tuna steak
4 tablespoons olive oil
Grated zest of 1 lime
3 tablespoons freshly squeezed lime juice
1/2 teaspoon wasabi powder
1 1/2 teaspoons soy sauce
6 dashes Tabasco sauce
1 1/2 teaspoons kosher salt
1 teaspoon freshly ground black pepper
1/4 cup minced scallions, white and green parts (2 scallions)
2 teaspoons minced fresh jalapeño pepper, seeds removed
1 ripe Hass avocado
1 teaspoon toasted sesame seeds (optional)

Cut the tuna into 1/4-inch dice and place it in a medium bowl. In a small bowl, combine the olive oil, lime zest, lime juice, wasabi, soy sauce, Tabasco, salt, and pepper. Pour over the tuna, add the scallions and jalapeño, and mix well. Cut the avocado in half, remove the seed, and peel. Cut the avocado into 1/4-inch dice. Carefully mix the avocado into the tuna mixture. Add the toasted sesame seeds if using and season to taste. Allow the mixture to sit in the refrigerator for at least an hour for the flavors to blend. Serve on crackers.

Use the finest quality tuna you can find; two of the best are yellowfin and big-eye.

Wasabi is a powder made from the dried root of Japanese horseradish. You can find this very pungent seasoning in the Asian section of the grocery store.

ARUGULA WITH PARMESAN

Serves 6

When I'm having a dinner party, I try not to cook more than two things; I'll assemble the rest. That way I don't spend the evening standing in front of the oven fretting, "Is it done?" This is an easy salad to assemble as a first course. The arugula is peppery, the vinaigrette lemony, and the Parmesan spicy. Prepare the ingredients in advance and just toss them together before dinner. Serve with a wedge of lemon if you like.

½ pound fresh arugula (3 large bunches)

LEMON VINAIGRETTE
¼ cup freshly squeezed lemon juice (2 lemons)
½ cup good olive oil
½ teaspoon kosher salt
¼ teaspoon freshly ground black pepper

¼-pound chunk very good Parmesan cheese

If the arugula has roots attached, cut them off. Fill the sink with cold water and toss the arugula for a few minutes to clean. Spin-dry the leaves and place them in a large bowl.

In a small bowl, whisk together the lemon juice, olive oil, salt, and pepper. Pour enough dressing on the arugula to moisten. Toss well and place the salad on individual plates.

With a very sharp knife or a vegetable peeler, shave the Parmesan into large shards and arrange them on the arugula.

Since this recipe has very few ingredients, it depends on using the best for its flavor. I always choose aged Italian Parmesan (Parmigiano-Reggiano) cheese.

GREEN SALAD WITH CREAMY MUSTARD VINAIGRETTE

Serves 6 to 8

When Alex Witchel, the talented New York Times *writer and novelist, came to interview me in East Hampton, it was a particularly miserable, cold, and rainy winter day. I served her a steaming bowl of lentil soup from* The Barefoot Contessa Cookbook, *a salad prepared with this vinaigrette, and a cheese board with Cheddar and Brie. It was a simple but warming lunch and we had a wonderful afternoon together. She graciously requested a copy of this recipe.*

> 3 tablespoons champagne vinegar
> 1/2 teaspoon Dijon mustard
> 1/2 teaspoon minced fresh garlic
> 1 extra-large egg yolk, at room temperature (see Note)
> 3/4 teaspoon kosher salt
> 1/4 teaspoon freshly ground black pepper
> 1/2 cup good olive oil
> Salad greens or mesclun mix for 6 to 8 people

In a small bowl, whisk together the vinegar, mustard, garlic, egg yolk, salt, and pepper. While whisking, slowly add the olive oil until the vinaigrette is emulsified.

Toss the greens with enough dressing to moisten and serve immediately.

If you're worried about raw egg, substitute 1 tablespoon mayonnaise.

When you're serving a salad for a dinner party, put the vinaigrette in the bottom of a serving bowl and place the greens on top. This can sit for an hour or two until you're ready to toss and serve it.

ENDIVE, STILTON & WALNUTS

Serves 6

This is a good salad to make in winter when endive is one of the only salad "greens" available. It's so easy to make and yet so elegant. You can make the vinaigrette several days in advance.

1 ½ pounds endive (5 heads)
1 cup walnut halves (3 ounces)
3 tablespoons white wine or champagne vinegar
1 teaspoon Dijon mustard
1 extra-large egg yolk, at room temperature (see Note)
1 teaspoon kosher salt
½ teaspoon freshly ground black pepper
½ cup good olive oil
6 to 8 ounces English Stilton cheese, crumbled
¼ cup whole fresh flat-leaf parsley leaves

Cut the end off each head of endive and peel or cut each leaf off the core. If the leaves are large, cut them in half lengthwise. Place the leaves in a large mixing bowl.

Toast the walnuts in a dry sauté pan over medium heat for about 3 minutes, tossing often, until warmed and crisp.

Whisk together the vinegar, mustard, egg yolk, salt, and pepper in a bowl. While whisking, slowly add the olive oil until the dressing is emulsified. Pour enough dressing onto the endive leaves to moisten and place them on individual plates. Sprinkle each salad with the crumbled Stilton, walnuts, and parsley leaves. Season to taste and serve.

If you're worried about eating raw egg yolk, substitute 1 tablespoon mayonnaise.

PARMESAN ROASTED ASPARAGUS

Serves 6

Italians often eat their vegetables as "antipasti," that is, before the main course. This is a very easy first course that I sometimes serve in the classic Italian way, topped with a single fried egg.

2 ½ pounds fresh asparagus (about 30 large)
2 tablespoons olive oil
½ teaspoon kosher salt
¼ teaspoon freshly ground black pepper
½ cup freshly grated Parmesan cheese
2 lemons cut in wedges, for serving

Preheat the oven to 400 degrees.

If the stalks of the asparagus are thick, peel the bottom half of each. Lay them in a single layer on a sheet pan and drizzle with olive oil. Sprinkle with salt and pepper. Roast for 15 to 20 minutes, until tender. Sprinkle with the Parmesan and return to the oven for another minute. Serve with lemon wedges.

I prefer thick asparagus to thin ones; they have much more flavor.

TURN UP THE VOLUME

We've all had the experience. We're invited to dinner at a friend's house. We ring the doorbell and the host (maybe a little distraught) opens the door to a VERY quiet house. Oops! Are we the first to arrive, or—worse—is it the wrong day? Either way, we feel a bit ill at ease and the evening's off to a bad start.

Replay the opening scene with this difference: the host opens the door and you hear Roy Orbison belting out "Pretty Woman" or the Beach Boys rocking to "Good Vibrations." Not only do you know you've come to a party, but you feel good immediately. No matter what kind of day you've had, your spirits soar. And that's a great start for a fabulous evening.

I think the first few minutes of a party really set the tone for the night. For me, music that makes you feel like you're at a party is the difference between a fun evening and a dull one. The music I choose is a lot like the food I make: it's familiar, but it's a little better than you remembered. I used to organize all the details for a party and then at the last minute throw some CDs on the stereo. Once I realized how important the music was, I started previewing my choices while I cooked dinner. (My CD changer holds six discs, more than enough for an entire evening.) During cocktails, I'll choose music that is upbeat and fun and I play it just a *little* too loud: Cesaria Evora's *Café Atlantico*, Stephane Pompougnac's *Costes: La Suite*, Pink Martini's *Sympathique*, and *The Best of the Temptations: Volume 1, the 60's*. I always know I'm successful if everyone is swaying to the music while we fix drinks and nibble on roasted cashews.

When it's time for dinner I want to turn down the volume a bit but I don't want something that's going to put everyone to sleep. This is a great time for Anita Baker's *Rapture*, Ann Hampton Callaway's *To Ella with Love*, and even something a little more emotional, like Roy Orbison's *For the Lonely*. The music makes you feel good but it's relaxed. Then, as I'm serving dessert and everyone is feeling *just* a little too satisfied, I'll crank up the volume again with something like Roxy Music's *Avalon* or a CD from the Cuban group Buena Vista Social Club. This way I'll send everyone home feeling upbeat and thinking, "Wasn't that fun!"

Lobster Cobb Salad, page 60

SALAD FOR LUNCH

Chicken WITH TABBOULEH

MONTAUK Seafood Salad

Pasta WITH SUN-DRIED TOMATOES

Lobster COBB SALAD

CURRIED Chicken Salad

BROWN RICE, Tomatoes & Basil

Tomato, MOZZARELLA & BASIL

Wheatberry SALAD

HERBAL Iced Tea

CHICKEN WITH TABBOULEH

Serves 6 to 8

Tabbouleh was always popular at Barefoot Contessa but I wanted to make it into a main course. I added diced roasted chicken and it was an immediate hit. Serve it as a first course for a summer dinner, for lunch in pita bread, or pack it in containers for a picnic at the beach.

1 ½ cups boiling water
1 cup bulgur wheat
¼ cup freshly squeezed lemon juice (2 lemons)
Olive oil
Kosher salt
1 whole (2 split) chicken breast, bone in, skin on
Freshly ground black pepper
1 cup minced scallions, white and green parts (1 bunch)
1 cup chopped fresh mint leaves (2 bunches)
1 cup chopped fresh flat-leaf parsley (1 bunch)
1 hothouse cucumber, unpeeled, halved lengthwise, seeded, and
  medium-diced
2 cups halved cherry tomatoes

Preheat the oven to 350 degrees.

In a heat-proof bowl, pour the boiling water over the bulgur wheat. Add the lemon juice, ¼ cup olive oil, and 1 ½ teaspoons of salt. Stir. Cover the bowl with plastic wrap and allow the bulgur to stand at room temperature for about an hour.

Place the chicken breast on a baking sheet and rub it with olive oil. Sprinkle liberally with salt and pepper. Roast for 35 to 40 minutes, until just cooked. Set aside until cool enough to handle.

Remove the chicken meat from the bones and discard the skin. Cut the chicken into medium dice and add to the tabbouleh. Add the scallions, mint, parsley, cucumber, tomatoes, 2 teaspoons salt, and 1 teaspoon pepper. Season to taste and serve immediately or cover and refrigerate. The flavors will improve as it sits.

There is no substitute for freshly squeezed lemon juice.

MONTAUK SEAFOOD SALAD

Serves 6

I know the Hamptons are associated with the rich and famous, but its heritage really derives from farming and fishing. Montauk, at the eastern tip of Long Island, is where the fishermen bring their catches, so we can have the freshest shellfish all year long.

FOR THE SEAFOOD
½ cup white wine vinegar
1 tablespoon kosher salt
1 ½ pounds large shrimp (25 to 30 shrimp), peeled and
    deveined
1 pound sea scallops (10 to 12)
3 pounds fresh mussels in the shell, scrubbed and beards
    removed

FOR THE SAUCE
1 cup good olive oil
½ teaspoon whole fresh thyme leaves
1 teaspoon minced fresh garlic
Zest of 2 lemons
¼ cup freshly squeezed lemon juice
1 teaspoon Dijon mustard
2 tablespoons champagne or white wine vinegar
2 teaspoons kosher salt
½ teaspoon freshly ground black pepper

TO ASSEMBLE
¾ cup medium-diced celery (2 stalks)
3 tablespoons chopped fresh parsley
Thinly sliced lemon, for garnish

To cook the seafood, combine 8 cups of water with the white wine vinegar and salt in a large saucepan and bring to a boil. Add the shrimp and cook for 2 minutes only. Remove with a slotted spoon. Bring the water back to a boil and cook the scallops for 4 to 5 minutes, until cooked through. Drain.

Bring ½ cup of water to a boil in the same saucepan and toss in the mussels. Return to a boil, cover, and steam for 3 to 5 minutes, until they're all opened. (Discard any that remain unopened after 5 minutes.) Drain. Remove the mussels from the shells and discard the shells. Drain all the cooked seafood and place it in a large bowl.

To make the sauce, heat the olive oil in a medium sauté pan and add the thyme, garlic, and lemon zest. Cook over low heat for 1 minute. Off the heat, add the lemon juice, mustard, vinegar, salt, and pepper. Pour the hot vinaigrette over the seafood.

Add the celery and parsley and toss well. This salad can be served immediately, but it is best when allowed to sit, refrigerated, for an hour or two. Sprinkle with salt and toss with sliced lemon.

PASTA WITH SUN-DRIED TOMATOES

Serves 6 to 8

I've been making this pasta for as long as I can remember. I think the original recipe came from my dear friend Brent Newsom, but we might have made some changes along the way. In any case, it's always one of the most popular summer salads at Barefoot Contessa.

½ pound fusilli (spirals) pasta
Kosher salt
Olive oil
1 pound ripe tomatoes, medium-diced
¾ cup good black olives, such as kalamata, pitted and diced
1 pound fresh mozzarella, medium-diced
6 sun-dried tomatoes in oil, drained and chopped

FOR THE DRESSING
5 sun-dried tomatoes in oil, drained
2 tablespoons red wine vinegar
6 tablespoons good olive oil
1 garlic clove, diced
1 teaspoon capers, drained
2 teaspoons kosher salt
¾ teaspoon freshly ground black pepper

1 cup freshly grated Parmesan cheese
1 cup packed basil leaves, julienned

Cook the pasta in a large pot of boiling salted water with a splash of oil to keep it from sticking together. Boil for 12 minutes, or according to the directions on the package. Drain well and allow to cool. Place the pasta in a bowl and add the tomatoes, olives, mozzarella, and chopped sun-dried tomatoes.

For the dressing, combine the sun-dried tomatoes, vinegar, olive oil, garlic, capers, salt, and pepper in a food processor until almost smooth.

Pour the dressing over the pasta, sprinkle with the Parmesan cheese and basil, and toss well.

This salad sits well, so you can make it early in the day. Add the Parmesan and basil just before serving.

LOBSTER COBB SALAD

Serves 4 to 6

Make this elegant salad when your mother-in-law comes for lunch—she'll love you. It's like a Cobb salad but with fresh lobster meat instead of chicken. Of course, you can always substitute cooked chicken or shrimp if you have a crowd, but this is a special meal for times when you really want to please someone.

FOR THE VINAIGRETTE
1 ½ tablespoons Dijon mustard
¼ cup freshly squeezed lemon juice (2 lemons)
5 tablespoons good olive oil
¾ teaspoon kosher salt
½ teaspoon freshly ground black pepper

FOR THE SALAD
2 ripe Hass avocados
Juice of 1 lemon
1 ½ pounds cooked lobster meat, cut in ¾-inch dice
1 pint cherry tomatoes, cut in half or quarters
1 ½ teaspoons kosher salt
½ teaspoon freshly ground black pepper
½ pound lean bacon, fried and crumbled
¾ cup crumbled English Stilton, or other crumbly blue cheese
1 bunch arugula, washed and spun dry

For the vinaigrette, whisk together the mustard, lemon juice, olive oil, salt, and pepper in a small bowl.

For the salad, cut the avocados in half, remove the seed, and peel. Cut into ¾-inch dice and toss with the lemon juice. If the arugula leaves are large, cut them in half crosswise.

Put the lobster and tomatoes in a bowl. Sprinkle with the salt and pepper and toss with enough vinaigrette to moisten. Add the diced avocados, crumbled bacon, blue cheese, and arugula and toss again. Serve at room temperature.

Hass avocados are the bumpy brown ones; they have more flavor than the bright green avocados. They're ripe when they give slightly to the touch.

CURRIED CHICKEN SALAD

Serves 6

Mimi Sheraton, the legendary New York Times *restaurant critic, used to say that the correct proportion of raisins to chicken in curried chicken salad is "none." I don't agree. This chicken salad has been offered at Barefoot Contessa for more than twenty years and customers would be cranky if we changed it. But make it your way—sweet or spicy and with or without raisins and cashews. The good news is that it's best made in advance, but add the cashews at the last minute so they stay crisp.*

3 whole (6 split) chicken breasts, bone in, skin on
Olive oil
Kosher salt
Freshly ground black pepper
1 ½ cups good mayonnaise
⅓ cup dry white wine
¼ cup Major Grey's chutney
3 tablespoons curry powder
1 cup medium-diced celery (2 large stalks)
¼ cup chopped scallions, white and green parts (2 scallions)
¼ cup raisins
1 cup whole roasted, salted cashews

Preheat the oven to 350 degrees.

Place the chicken breasts on a sheet pan and rub the skin with olive oil. Sprinkle liberally with salt and pepper. Roast for 35 to 40 minutes, until the chicken is just cooked. Set aside until cool enough to handle. Remove the meat from the bones, discard the skin, and dice the chicken in large bite-size pieces.

For the dressing, combine the mayonnaise, wine, chutney, curry powder, and 1 ½ teaspoons salt in the bowl of a food processor fitted with the steel blade. Process until smooth.

Combine the chicken with enough dressing to moisten well. Add the celery, scallions, and raisins, and mix well. Refrigerate for a few hours to allow the flavors to blend. Add the cashews and serve at room temperature.

To roast cashews, place them in a dry sauté pan over medium-low heat and stir until they're a little crisp, about 5 minutes.

BROWN RICE, TOMATOES & BASIL

Serves 6

This salad was inspired by a recipe in The Loaves and Fishes Cookbook *written by my dear friend Anna Pump. She and her daughter Sybille own a wonderful specialty food store by the same name in Sagaponack, New York. I think brown rice gives the salad a nutty, wholesome flavor.*

1 cup Texmati brown rice
2 teaspoons kosher salt, divided
¼ cup champagne or rice wine vinegar
2 teaspoons sugar
1 tablespoon good olive oil
Freshly ground black pepper
1 pound ripe tomatoes, large-diced
1 cup packed basil leaves (1 large bunch), chopped
   (see Note, page 64)

Bring 2¼ cups water to a boil and add the rice and 1 teaspoon of the salt. Return to a boil, cover, and simmer for 30 to 40 minutes, until the rice is tender and all the water is absorbed. Transfer the rice to a bowl.

Whisk together the vinegar, sugar, olive oil, remaining teaspoon of salt, and a pinch of pepper. Pour over the rice. Add the tomatoes and basil. Mix well and check the seasonings. Serve at room temperature.

If your stove is hot, keep the pan half off the burner.

To make this salad a day ahead, omit the basil. Before serving, check the seasonings and add the chopped fresh basil.

TOMATO, MOZZARELLA & BASIL

Serves 6 to 8

The simplicity of this dish requires the best ingredients: summer tomatoes, freshly made mozzarella, and garden basil. This is just a more casual way to prepare the traditional "Caprese" salad for a crowd.

6 small tomatoes (4 medium)
1 pound fresh mozzarella
10 to 15 basil leaves
3 tablespoons good olive oil
Kosher salt
Freshly ground black pepper

Slice the tomatoes and mozzarella and arrange with the basil leaves on a large platter. Drizzle with olive oil. Sprinkle with salt and pepper and serve at room temperature.

To clean basil, remove the leaves from the stems, wash them in a bowl of water, and then spin them very dry in a salad spinner. Store them in the refrigerator in a closed plastic bag with a dry paper towel. They will stay green for several days.

WHEATBERRY SALAD

Serves 6

My friend Brent Newsom devised this hearty salad. Wheatberries are a nutty grain that we use to make breads and salads. There are several different types, but hard winter wheatberries don't get mushy when they're cooked. If you can't find them in the grocery store, try your local health-food store. They're delicious, and so good for you!

> 1 cup hard winter wheatberries
> Kosher salt
> 1 cup finely diced red onion (1 onion)
> 6 tablespoons good olive oil, divided
> 2 tablespoons balsamic vinegar
> 3 scallions, minced, white and green parts
> ½ red bell pepper, small-diced
> 1 carrot, small-diced
> ½ teaspoon freshly ground black pepper

Place the wheatberries and 3 cups of boiling salted water in a saucepan and cook, uncovered, over low heat for approximately 45 minutes, or until they are soft. Drain.

Sauté the red onion in 2 tablespoons of olive oil over medium-low heat until translucent, approximately 5 minutes. Turn off the heat and add the remaining 4 tablespoons (¼ cup) of olive oil and the balsamic vinegar.

In a large bowl, combine the warm wheatberries, sautéed onions, scallions, red bell pepper, carrot, ½ teaspoon salt, and the pepper. Allow the salad to sit for at least 30 minutes for the wheatberries to absorb the sauce. Season to taste and serve at room temperature.

HERBAL ICED TEA

Serves 6 to 8

On a ski trip to Aspen one year, my husband Jeffrey and I ordered iced tea at a terrific restaurant called Main Street Cafe and Bakery. I never found out what was in it, but I think this is close. Barefoot Contessa sells gallons of it every day during the summer. The good news is that it doesn't have any caffeine and it doesn't need any sugar; the apple juice sweetens it naturally.

4 Celestial Seasonings Lemon Zinger tea bags
4 Celestial Seasonings Red Zinger tea bags
4 cups pure apple juice

Steep the 8 tea bags in 4 cups of boiling water for about 10 minutes. Discard the tea bags. Combine the tea with the apple juice and refrigerate until cold. Serve over ice.

I use Martinelli's pure apple juice.

Penne with Five Cheeses, page 89

DINNERS

HERB-ROASTED Lamb

Sunday Rib Roast WITH MUSTARD HORSERADISH SAUCE

OVEN-FRIED Chicken

Parmesan CHICKEN

TEQUILA LIME Chicken

Saffron Risotto WITH BUTTERNUT SQUASH

Penne WITH FIVE CHEESES

Chicken Stew WITH BISCUITS

SCOTT'S Short Ribs

PARKER'S Fish & Chips

Lasagna WITH TURKEY SAUSAGE

REAL MEATBALLS & Spaghetti

Linguine WITH SHRIMP SCAMPI

HERB-ROASTED LAMB

Serves 10

Doesn't it sound delicious to roast a rosemary leg of lamb over a bed of potatoes so the juices of the lamb flavor the potatoes while they cook? The best part is that the whole dish goes into the oven almost two hours before dinner so you can actually relax before your guests arrive. Have the butcher remove the leg bone but leave the shank intact.

12 large unpeeled garlic cloves, divided
1 tablespoon chopped fresh rosemary leaves
Kosher salt
Freshly ground black pepper
2 tablespoons unsalted butter, melted
1 6-pound boneless leg of lamb, trimmed and tied
4 to 5 pounds small unpeeled potatoes (16 to 20 potatoes)
2 tablespoons good olive oil

Preheat the oven to 450 degrees. Place the oven rack in the lower third of the oven so the lamb will sit in the middle of the oven.

Peel 6 of the cloves of garlic and place them in the bowl of a food processor fitted with the steel blade. Add the rosemary, 1 tablespoon salt, 1 teaspoon pepper, and butter. Process until the garlic and rosemary are finely minced. Thoroughly coat the top and sides of the lamb with the rosemary mixture. Allow to sit at room temperature for 30 minutes to an hour.

Toss the potatoes and remaining unpeeled garlic in a bowl with the olive oil and sprinkle with salt. Place in the bottom of a large roasting pan. Place the lamb on top of the potatoes and roast for 1¼ to 1½ hours, or until the internal temperature of the lamb is 135 degrees (rare) or 145 degrees (medium). Remove from the oven and put the lamb on a platter; cover tightly with aluminum foil. Allow the lamb to rest for about 20 minutes. Slice and serve with the potatoes.

Fresh rosemary is important for this dish.

It's not easy to know when the lamb has reached the right temperature. I use an instant-read thermometer and stick it in 4 or 5 places near the middle of the leg of lamb to make sure that none of the meat at the center is below the desired temperature.

SUNDAY RIB ROAST

Serves 6 to 8

Remember the old Burns and Allen skit where Gracie tells George how she makes roast beef? "Well," she'd say, "I put two roasts in the oven; a little one and a big one. When the little one is burnt, then I know the big one is done." Sometimes I feel like Gracie trying to figure out if the roast is done, but this system from Barbara Kafka's Roasting *seems to produce a perfect rib roast every time—rare in the middle and medium-rare on the ends. When I cook at 500 degrees I make sure my oven is perfectly clean; otherwise it creates a lot of smoke.*

> 1 3-rib standing rib roast (7 to 8 pounds)
> 1 tablespoon kosher salt
> 1½ teaspoons freshly ground black pepper
> Mustard Horseradish Sauce or Stilton Sauce (recipes follow)

Two hours before roasting, remove the meat from the refrigerator and allow it to come to room temperature.

Preheat the oven to 500 degrees. Place the oven rack on the second lowest position.

Place the roast in a pan large enough to hold it comfortably, bones side down, and spread the top thickly with the salt and pepper. Roast the meat for 45 minutes. Without removing the meat from the oven, reduce the oven temperature to 325 degrees and roast for another 30 minutes. Finally, increase the temperature to 450 degrees and roast for another 15 to 30 minutes, until the internal temperature of the meat is 125 degrees. (Be sure the thermometer is exactly in the center of the roast.) The total cooking time will be between 1½ and 1¾ hours.

Remove the roast from the oven and transfer it to a cutting board. Cover it tightly with aluminum foil and allow the meat to rest for 20 minutes. Carve and serve with the sauce.

An instant-read thermometer is very helpful for this recipe.

Don't allow the meat to sit covered with aluminum foil for more than 30 minutes or it will overcook!

Mustard Horseradish Sauce

Serves 6 to 8

1 ½ cups good mayonnaise
3 tablespoons Dijon mustard
1 ½ tablespoons whole-grain mustard
1 tablespoon prepared horseradish
⅓ cup sour cream
¼ teaspoon kosher salt

Whisk together the mayonnaise, mustards, horseradish, sour cream, and salt in a small bowl. Serve at room temperature.

Stilton Sauce

Serves 6 to 8

4 ounces Stilton cheese, crumbled
8 ounces cream cheese, at room temperature
½ cup good mayonnaise
½ cup sour cream
1 tablespoon chopped scallions, white and green parts
1 teaspoon kosher salt
½ teaspoon freshly ground black pepper
¼ teaspoon Worcestershire sauce

Place the Stilton in the bowl of a food processor fitted with a steel blade and blend until finely minced. Add the cream cheese, mayonnaise, sour cream, scallions, salt, pepper, and Worcestershire sauce. Process until smooth. Serve at room temperature.

OVEN-FRIED CHICKEN

Serves 6

Everyone loves fried chicken. I wanted to find a way to fry it in advance so I wasn't standing at the stove, covered in grease, while everyone waited for dinner. Parker Hodges at Barefoot Contessa solved the problem brilliantly. Now I fry each piece for about 10 minutes, and then cook the chicken on a baking rack in the oven, which makes it crisp on the outside and tender and juicy inside. It's so much easier and you don't need to scour the kitchen after you're done! Just remember that the chicken needs to marinate overnight.

2 chickens (3 pounds each), cut in eight serving pieces
1 quart buttermilk
2 cups all-purpose flour
1 tablespoon kosher salt
1 tablespoon freshly ground black pepper
Vegetable oil or vegetable shortening

Place the chicken pieces in a large bowl and pour the buttermilk over them. Cover with plastic wrap and refrigerate overnight.

Preheat the oven to 350 degrees.

Combine the flour, salt, and pepper in a large bowl. Take the chicken out of the buttermilk and coat each piece thoroughly with the flour mixture. Pour the oil into a large heavy-bottomed stockpot to a depth of 1 inch and heat to 360 degrees on a thermometer.

Working in batches, carefully place several pieces of chicken in the oil and fry for about 3 minutes on each side until the coating is a light golden brown (it will continue to brown in the oven). Don't crowd the pieces. Remove the chicken from the oil and place each piece on a metal baking rack set on a sheet pan. Allow the oil to return to 360 degrees before frying the next batch. When all the chicken is fried, bake for 30 to 40 minutes, until the chicken is no longer pink inside. Serve hot.

Most people use a frying pan, but I prefer a stockpot so the hot grease doesn't get all over the stove (and me!).

I use a candy thermometer to check the oil temperature.

PARMESAN CHICKEN

Serves 6

My favorite restaurant in Milan is Bice. It's the kind of place where elegant Italian men nibble the fingers of incredibly chic Italian women. I often order the pan-roasted veal chop with a salad on top. I tried something similar with chicken and it turned out to be a staple in our house. I love the interplay of the hot and piquant chicken with the cold, citrusy salad. Because you'll need to cook the chicken in two batches (or use two skillets), this is not a good choice for a big crowd.

6 boneless, skinless chicken breasts
1 cup all-purpose flour
1 teaspoon kosher salt
½ teaspoon freshly ground black pepper
2 extra-large eggs
1¼ cups seasoned dry bread crumbs
½ cup freshly grated Parmesan cheese, plus extra for serving
Unsalted butter
Good olive oil
Salad greens for 6, washed and spun dry
Lemon Vinaigrette (see page 40)

Pound the chicken breasts until they are ¼ inch thick. You can use either a meat mallet or a rolling pin.

Combine the flour, salt, and pepper on a dinner plate. On a second plate, beat the eggs with 1 tablespoon of water. On a third plate, combine the bread crumbs and ½ cup grated Parmesan cheese. Coat the chicken breasts on both sides with the flour mixture, then dip both sides into the egg mixture and dredge both sides in the bread-crumb mixture, pressing lightly.

Heat 1 tablespoon of butter and 1 tablespoon of olive oil in a large sauté pan and cook 2 or 3 chicken breasts on medium-low heat for 2 to 3 minutes on each side, until cooked through. Add more butter and oil and cook the rest of the chicken breasts. Toss the salad greens with lemon vinaigrette. Place a mound of salad on each hot chicken breast. Serve with extra grated Parmesan.

You can pound the meat between two sheets of wax paper or plastic wrap.

Keep the chicken breasts warm for about 15 minutes on a sheet pan in a 200-degree oven.

TEQUILA LIME CHICKEN

Serves 6

In warm weather, this chicken flies out of Barefoot Contessa. We can buy boneless chicken breasts with the skin on, but if you can't get them that way, just buy chicken breasts on the bone and run a sharp knife between the meat and the bone to separate them. It takes a bit of skill but the technique is easy to learn.

½ cup gold tequila
1 cup freshly squeezed lime juice (5 to 6 limes)
½ cup freshly squeezed orange juice (2 oranges)
1 tablespoon chili powder
1 tablespoon minced fresh jalapeño pepper (1 pepper seeded)
1 tablespoon minced fresh garlic (3 cloves)
2 teaspoons kosher salt
1 teaspoon freshly ground black pepper
3 whole (6 split) boneless chicken breasts, skin on

Combine the tequila, lime juice, orange juice, chili powder, jalapeño pepper, garlic, salt, and pepper in a large bowl. Add the chicken breasts. Refrigerate overnight.

Heat a grill with coals and brush the rack with oil to prevent the chicken from sticking. Remove the chicken breasts from the marinade, sprinkle well with salt and pepper, and grill them skin-side down for about 5 minutes, until nicely browned. Turn the chicken and cook for another 10 minutes, until just cooked through. Remove from the grill to a plate. Cover tightly and allow to rest for 5 minutes. Serve hot or at room temperature.

If you like cilantro, add 1 tablespoon, minced, to the marinade.

I use Cuervo Gold tequila.

There is no substitute for freshly squeezed lime juice.

SAFFRON RISOTTO
WITH BUTTERNUT SQUASH

Serves 4 to 6

I used to avoid risotto because I thought you had to stand by the stove for hours, stirring—not exactly my style! But, I decided to give it a try and, instead, found a dish that's so delicious and cooks in 30 minutes. Test this first on your family and then when you have a party, you can invite your guests into the kitchen for drinks while everyone takes turns stirring the risotto.

1 butternut squash (2 pounds)
2 tablespoons olive oil
Kosher salt
Freshly ground black pepper
6 cups chicken stock, preferably homemade (page 93)
6 tablespoons (¾ stick) unsalted butter
2 ounces pancetta, diced
½ cup minced shallots (2 large)
1½ cups Arborio rice (10 ounces)
½ cup dry white wine
1 teaspoon saffron threads
1 cup freshly grated Parmesan cheese

Preheat the oven to 400 degrees.

Peel the butternut squash, remove the seeds, and cut it into ¾-inch cubes. You should have about 6 cups. Place the squash on a sheet pan and toss it with the olive oil, 1 teaspoon salt, and ½ teaspoon pepper. Roast for 25 to 30 minutes, tossing once, until very tender. Set aside.

Meanwhile, heat the chicken stock in a small covered saucepan. Leave it on low heat to simmer.

In a heavy-bottomed pot or Dutch oven, melt the butter and sauté the pancetta and shallots on medium-low heat for 10 minutes, until the shallots are translucent but not browned. Add the rice and stir to coat the grains with butter. Add the wine and cook for 2 minutes. Add 2 full ladles of stock to the rice plus the saffron, 1 teaspoon salt, and ½ teaspoon pepper. Stir, and simmer until the stock is absorbed, 5 to 10 minutes. Continue to add the

stock, 2 ladles at a time, stirring every few minutes. Each time, cook until the mixture seems a little dry, then add more stock. Continue until the rice is cooked through, but still al dente, about 30 minutes total. Off the heat, add the roasted squash cubes and Parmesan cheese. Mix well and serve.

Marcella Hazan advises that correct heat is important in making risotto. It should be "lively"; too high heat and the grains don't cook evenly, and too low heat will result in a gluey mess. It should cook in 30 minutes. After the first try, you'll get the idea.

Saffron is collected from the stamens of crocuses, which is why it's so expensive. Use the strands, not the powder.

Pancetta is Italian bacon. If you can't find it, use any good-quality bacon.

PENNE WITH FIVE CHEESES

Serves 6

This recipe comes from George Germon and Johanne Killeen and their wonderful cookbook Cucina Simpatica. *They own the award-winning restaurant in Providence, Rhode Island, called Al Forno, and we make pilgrimages there from time to time. This dish is easy to make for your family but elegant enough to serve to company.*

Kosher salt
2 cups heavy cream
1 cup crushed tomatoes in thick tomato puree
½ cup freshly grated Pecorino Romano (1½ ounces)
½ cup shredded imported Italian fontina (1½ ounces)
¼ cup crumbled Italian Gorgonzola (1½ ounces)
2 tablespoons ricotta cheese
¼ pound fresh mozzarella, sliced
6 fresh basil leaves, chopped
1 pound imported penne rigate pasta
4 tablespoons (½ stick) unsalted butter

Preheat the oven to 500 degrees.

Bring 5 quarts of salted water to a boil in a stockpot.

Combine all the ingredients except the penne and butter in a large mixing bowl. Mix well.

Drop the penne into the boiling water and parboil for 4 minutes. Drain well in a colander and add to the ingredients in the mixing bowl, tossing to combine.

Divide the pasta mixture among 6 shallow ceramic gratin dishes (1½- to 2-cup capacity). Dot with the butter and bake until bubbly and brown on top, 7 to 10 minutes.

This is a very versatile recipe; even George and Johanne make lots of variations. I like to double the Gorgonzola and add ½ cup of grated Parmesan cheese.

I use Redpack crushed tomatoes.

CHICKEN STEW WITH BISCUITS

Serves 8

I'm a big believer in recipes that can be served in lots of ways. It takes the stress out of cooking when I know how to make a dish. This is essentially the filling for a chicken pot pie topped with home-made biscuits; you can substitute any pot pie filling, such as the one for lobster pot pie (The Bare-foot Contessa Cookbook) or vegetable pot pie (Barefoot Contessa Parties!).

FOR THE STEW

3 whole (6 split) chicken breasts, bone in, skin on
3 tablespoons olive oil
Kosher salt and freshly ground black pepper
5 cups chicken stock, preferably homemade (page 93)
2 chicken bouillon cubes
12 tablespoons (1½ sticks) unsalted butter
2 cups chopped yellow onions (2 onions)
¾ cup all-purpose flour
¼ cup heavy cream
2 cups medium-diced carrots (4 carrots), blanched for 2 minutes
1 10-ounce package frozen peas (2 cups)
1½ cups frozen small whole onions
½ cup minced fresh parsley

FOR THE BISCUITS

2 cups all-purpose flour
1 tablespoon baking powder
1 teaspoon kosher salt
1 teaspoon sugar
¼ pound (1 stick) cold unsalted butter, diced
¾ cup half-and-half
½ cup chopped fresh parsley
1 egg mixed with 1 tablespoon water, for egg wash

Preheat the oven to 375 degrees.

Place the chicken breasts on a sheet pan and rub them with olive oil. Sprinkle generously with salt and pepper. Roast for 35 to 40 minutes, or until cooked through. Set aside until cool enough to handle, then remove the

meat from the bones and discard the skin. Cut the chicken into large dice. You will have 4 to 6 cups of cubed chicken.

In a small saucepan, heat the chicken stock and dissolve the bouillon cubes in the stock. In a large pot or Dutch oven, melt the butter and sauté the onions over medium-low heat for 10 to 15 minutes, until translucent. Add the flour and cook over low heat, stirring constantly, for 2 minutes. Add the hot chicken stock to the sauce. Simmer over low heat for 1 more minute, stirring, until thick. Add 2 teaspoons salt, ½ teaspoon pepper, and the heavy cream. Add the cubed chicken, carrots, peas, onions, and parsley. Mix well. Place the stew in a 10 × 13 × 2-inch oval or rectangular baking dish. Place the baking dish on a sheet pan lined with parchment or wax paper. Bake for 15 minutes.

Meanwhile, make the biscuits. Combine the flour, baking powder, salt, and sugar in the bowl of an electric mixer fitted with the paddle attachment. Add the butter and mix on low speed until the butter is the size of peas. Add the half-and-half and combine on low speed. Mix in the parsley.

Dump the dough out on a well-floured board and, with a rolling pin, roll out to ⅜ inch thick. Cut out twelve circles with a 2½-inch round cutter.

Remove the stew from the oven and arrange the biscuits on top of the filling. Brush them with egg wash, and return the dish to the oven. Bake for another 20 to 30 minutes, until the biscuits are brown and the stew is bubbly.

To make in advance, refrigerate the chicken stew and biscuits separately. Bake the stew for 25 minutes, then place the biscuits on top, and bake for another 30 minutes, until done.

Chicken Stock

Makes 6 quarts

3 5-pound roasting chickens
3 large yellow onions, unpeeled, quartered
6 carrots, unpeeled, halved
4 celery stalks with leaves, cut in thirds
4 parsnips, unpeeled, cut in half (optional)
20 sprigs fresh parsley
15 sprigs fresh thyme
20 sprigs fresh dill
1 head garlic, unpeeled, cut in half crosswise
2 tablespoons kosher salt
2 teaspoons whole black peppercorns

Place the chickens, onions, carrots, celery, parsnips, parsley, thyme, dill, garlic, and seasonings in a 16- to 20-quart stockpot. Add 7 quarts of water and bring to a boil. Simmer uncovered for 4 hours. Strain the entire contents of the pot through a colander and discard the solids. Chill the stock overnight. The next day, remove the surface fat. Use immediately or pack in containers and freeze for up to 3 months.

SCOTT'S SHORT RIBS

Serves 6

Scott Bieber is the wonderful chef at Eli's Manhattan restaurant in New York City. He cooks earthy food that brings out the essence of the ingredients, such as these short ribs. You can make them well in advance and reheat them before dinner.

6 beef short ribs, trimmed of fat
Kosher salt
Freshly ground black pepper
¼ cup good olive oil
1½ cups chopped onion (2 onions)
4 cups large-diced celery (6 large stalks)
2 carrots, peeled and large-diced
1 small fennel, fronds, stems, and core removed, large-diced
1 leek, cleaned and large-diced, white part only
3 garlic cloves, finely chopped
1 750-ml bottle burgundy or other dry red wine
Fresh rosemary sprigs
Fresh thyme sprigs
6 cups beef stock
1 tablespoon brown sugar

Preheat the oven to 400 degrees. Place the short ribs on a sheet pan, sprinkle with salt and pepper, and roast for 15 minutes. Remove from the oven. Reduce the oven temperature to 300 degrees.

Meanwhile, heat the olive oil in a large Dutch oven and add the onion, celery, carrots, fennel, and leek and cook over medium-low heat for 20 minutes, stirring occasionally. Add the garlic and cook for another 2 minutes. Pour the wine over the vegetables, bring to a boil, and cook over high heat until the liquid is reduced by half, about 10 minutes. Add 1 tablespoon salt and 1 teaspoon pepper. Tie the rosemary and thyme together with kitchen twine and add to the pot.

Place the roasted ribs on top of the vegetables in the Dutch oven and add the beef stock and brown sugar. Bring to a simmer over high heat. Cover the Dutch oven and bake for 2 hours or until the meat is very tender.

Carefully remove the short ribs from the pot and set aside. Discard the herbs and skim the excess fat. Cook the vegetables and sauce over medium heat for 20 minutes, until reduced. Put the ribs back into the pot and heat through. Serve with the vegetables and sauce.

I use a reasonably priced Côtes du Rhône wine.

PARKER'S FISH & CHIPS

Serves 6

Parker Hodges, the chef and co-owner of Barefoot Contessa, decided to serve hot lunches during the winter and he told me that his fish & chips was the first thing to run out. I love that the "chips" are baked!

> 3 pounds fresh cod fillets (choose thick ones)
> Kosher salt
> Freshly ground black pepper
> 1 cup plus 2 tablespoons all-purpose flour
> 1 tablespoon baking powder
> 1 teaspoon freshly grated lemon zest
> ¼ teaspoon cayenne pepper
> 2 extra-large eggs
> Vegetable oil
> Baked "Chips" (recipe follows)

Lay the cod fillets on a cutting board. Sprinkle both sides with salt and pepper. Cut the fillets in 1½ × 3-inch pieces.

In a bowl, combine the flour, baking powder, lemon zest, cayenne pepper, 1½ teaspoons salt, and ¾ teaspoon pepper. Whisk in 1 cup of water and then the 2 eggs.

Pour ½ inch of oil into a large (12-inch) frying pan and heat it to about 360 degrees. Dip each fillet into the batter, allowing the excess to drip back into the bowl. Place it very carefully into the hot oil. Don't crowd the pieces. Adjust the heat as needed to keep the oil between 360 and 400 degrees. Cook the fish on each side for 2 to 3 minutes, until lightly browned and cooked through. Remove to a plate lined with a paper towel. Sprinkle with salt and serve hot with the "chips."

To keep hot for up to 20 minutes, line a baking sheet with paper towels and put the fish into a 200-degree oven.

Baked "Chips"

Serves 6

These are so good that you shouldn't have to wait for fish & chips to make them. They're great any time you want to serve crisp potatoes without the frying. Especially when they're made with garlic and rosemary, I'll bet you can't eat just one!

4 large baking potatoes, unpeeled
4 tablespoons good olive oil
1½ teaspoons kosher salt
¾ teaspoon freshly ground black pepper
1 teaspoon minced fresh garlic
1 teaspoon minced fresh rosemary leaves

Preheat the oven to 400 degrees.

Scrub the potatoes, cut them in half lengthwise, then cut each half in thirds lengthwise. You'll have six long wedges from each potato. Place the potatoes on a sheet pan with the olive oil, salt, pepper, garlic, and rosemary. With clean hands, toss all the ingredients together, making sure the potatoes are covered with oil. Spread the potatoes in a single layer with one cut side down.

Bake the potatoes for 30 to 35 minutes, turning to the other cut side after 20 minutes. Bake until they are lightly browned, crisp outside, and tender inside. Sprinkle with salt and serve immediately.

If you don't have fresh rosemary, these chips are delicious with just olive oil, salt, pepper, and garlic.

LASAGNA WITH TURKEY SAUSAGE

Serves 8

Everyone has a favorite family lasagna recipe. I wanted to make one that was lighter—with turkey sausage—and easier: we don't precook the lasagna noodles! My friends demanded the recipe after I made it for them. You can even assemble this a day ahead and bake it right before dinner.

2 tablespoons olive oil
1 cup chopped yellow onion (1 onion)
2 garlic cloves, minced
1½ pounds sweet Italian turkey sausage, casings removed
1 28-ounce can crushed tomatoes in tomato puree
1 6-ounce can tomato paste
¼ cup chopped fresh flat-leaf parsley, divided
½ cup chopped fresh basil leaves
Kosher salt
Freshly ground black pepper
½ pound lasagna noodles
15 ounces ricotta cheese
3 to 4 ounces creamy goat cheese, crumbled
1 cup grated Parmesan cheese, plus ¼ cup for sprinkling
1 extra-large egg, lightly beaten
1 pound fresh mozzarella, thinly sliced

Preheat the oven to 400 degrees.

Heat the olive oil in a large (10- to 12-inch) skillet. Add the onion and cook for 5 minutes over medium-low heat, until translucent. Add the garlic and cook for 1 more minute. Add the sausage and cook over medium-low heat, breaking it up with a fork, for 8 to 10 minutes, or until no longer pink. Add the tomatoes, tomato paste, 2 tablespoons of the parsley, the basil, 1½ teaspoons salt, and ½ teaspoon pepper. Simmer, uncovered, over medium-low heat, for 15 to 20 minutes, until thickened.

Meanwhile, fill a large bowl with the hottest tap water. Add the noodles and allow them to sit in the water for 20 minutes. Drain.

In a medium bowl, combine the ricotta, goat cheese, 1 cup of Parmesan, the

egg, the remaining 2 tablespoons of parsley, ½ teaspoon salt, and ¼ teaspoon pepper. Set aside.

Ladle ⅓ of the sauce into a 9 × 12 × 2-inch rectangular baking dish, spreading the sauce over the bottom of the dish. Then add the layers as follows: half the pasta, half the mozzarella, half the ricotta, and one third of the sauce. Add the rest of the pasta, mozzarella, ricotta, and finally, sauce. Sprinkle with ¼ cup of Parmesan cheese. Bake for 30 minutes, until the sauce is bubbling.

I use Shady Brook Farms' sweet Italian turkey sausage; you can also use their hot Italian turkey sausage, if you prefer.

To make ahead, refrigerate the assembled, unbaked lasagna. Bake for 30 to 40 minutes, until bubbly.

REAL MEATBALLS & SPAGHETTI

Serves 6

This is not something my mother made when I was growing up, so I had to do some research about spaghetti and meatballs. The best idea came from the famous New York Italian restaurant called Rao's: they add water to the meatballs, which keeps them moist and delicious. I may not be Italian, but this has definitely become a staple in my house.

FOR THE MEATBALLS

½ pound ground veal

½ pound ground pork

1 pound ground beef

1 cup fresh white bread crumbs (4 slices, crusts removed)

¼ cup seasoned dry bread crumbs

2 tablespoons chopped fresh flat-leaf parsley

½ cup freshly grated Parmesan cheese

2 teaspoons kosher salt

½ teaspoon freshly ground black pepper

¼ teaspoon ground nutmeg

1 extra-large egg, beaten

Vegetable oil

Olive oil

FOR THE SAUCE

1 tablespoon good olive oil

1 cup chopped yellow onion (1 onion)

1½ teaspoons minced garlic

½ cup good red wine, such as Chianti

1 28-ounce can crushed tomatoes, or plum tomatoes in puree, chopped

1 tablespoon chopped fresh flat-leaf parsley

1½ teaspoons kosher salt

½ teaspoon freshly ground black pepper

FOR SERVING

1½ pounds spaghetti, cooked according to package directions

Freshly grated Parmesan cheese

Place the ground meats, both bread crumbs, parsley, Parmesan, salt, pepper, nutmeg, egg, and ¾ cup warm water in a bowl. Combine very lightly with a fork. Using your hands, lightly form the mixture into 2-inch meatballs. You will have 14 to 16 meatballs.

Pour equal amounts of vegetable oil and olive oil into a large (12-inch) skillet to a depth of ¼ inch. Heat the oil. Very carefully, in batches, place the meatballs in the oil and brown them well on all sides over medium-low heat, turning carefully with a spatula or a fork. This should take about 10 minutes for each batch. Don't crowd the meatballs. Remove the meatballs to a plate covered with paper towels. Discard the oil but don't clean the pan.

For the sauce, heat the olive oil in the same pan. Add the onion and sauté over medium heat until translucent, 5 to 10 minutes. Add the garlic and cook for 1 more minute. Add the wine and cook on high heat, scraping up all the brown bits in the pan, until almost all the liquid evaporates, about 3 minutes. Stir in the tomatoes, parsley, salt, and pepper.

Return the meatballs to the sauce, cover, and simmer on the lowest heat for 25 to 30 minutes, until the meatballs are cooked through. Serve hot on cooked spaghetti and pass the grated Parmesan cheese.

When you cook spaghetti, don't use oil in the water; the sauce will stick better.

When the spaghetti is cooked, drain it in a colander. If you don't use it right away, run hot water over it and it will separate.

I use Pepperidge Farm sandwich white bread for fresh bread crumbs.

LINGUINE WITH SHRIMP SCAMPI

Serves 6

I wrote this recipe for my column in Martha Stewart Living *magazine called "Entertaining Is Fun." Except for the shrimp, you probably have most of the ingredients around the house and when you're late from work, it's a quick meal to pull together for dinner. Buy peeled and deveined shrimp and it's even faster!*

Vegetable oil
Kosher salt
1½ pounds linguine
6 tablespoons (¾ stick) unsalted butter
5 tablespoons good olive oil
3 tablespoons minced garlic (9 cloves)
2 pounds large shrimp (about 32 shrimp), peeled and deveined
½ teaspoon freshly ground black pepper
¾ cup chopped fresh parsley
Grated zest of 1 lemon
½ cup freshly squeezed lemon juice (4 lemons)
½ lemon, thinly sliced in half-rounds
¼ teaspoon hot red pepper flakes

Drizzle some oil in a large pot of boiling salted water, add 1 tablespoon of salt and the linguine, and cook for 7 to 10 minutes, or according to the directions on the package.

Meanwhile, in another large (12-inch), heavy-bottomed pan, melt the butter and olive oil over medium-low heat. Add the garlic. Sauté for 1 minute. Be careful, the garlic burns easily! Add the shrimp, 1 tablespoon of salt, and the pepper and sauté until the shrimp have just turned pink, about 5 minutes, stirring often. Remove from the heat, add the parsley, lemon zest, lemon juice, lemon slices, and red pepper flakes. Toss to combine.

When the pasta is done, drain the cooked linguine and then put it back in the pot. Immediately add the shrimp and sauce, toss well, and serve.

VEGETABLES

ROASTED Winter Vegetables

MASHED Yellow Turnips
WITH CRISPY SHALLOTS

String Beans WITH SHALLOTS

PROVENÇAL Tomatoes

Mashed Potatoes & GRAVY

Zucchini WITH PARMESAN

SAUTÉED Carrots

GARLIC SAUTÉED Spinach

MASHED Butternut Squash

Sagaponack Corn PUDDING

Wild Rice PILAF

ROSEMARY Polenta

ROASTED WINTER VEGETABLES

Serves 8

This is my favorite way to cook vegetables. The high temperature caramelizes the outside and leaves the inside tender and moist. This is a very flexible recipe; you can add any root vegetable you have in the house to this mélange.

> 1 pound carrots, peeled
> 1 pound parsnips, peeled
> 1 large sweet potato, peeled
> 1 small butternut squash (about 2 pounds), peeled and seeded
> 3 tablespoons good olive oil
> 1 ½ teaspoons kosher salt
> ½ teaspoon freshly ground black pepper
> 2 tablespoons chopped fresh flat-leaf parsley

Preheat the oven to 425 degrees.

Cut the carrots, parsnips, sweet potato, and butternut squash in 1- to 1 ¼-inch cubes. All the vegetables will shrink while baking, so don't cut them too small.

Place all the cut vegetables in a single layer on two sheet pans. Drizzle them with olive oil, salt, and pepper. Toss well. Bake for 25 to 35 minutes, until all the vegetables are tender, turning once with a metal spatula.

Sprinkle with parsley, season to taste, and serve hot.

Use the leftovers to make Roasted Vegetable Soup (page 33).

MASHED YELLOW TURNIPS
WITH CRISPY SHALLOTS

Serves 6

Danny Meyer's first of many successful restaurants in New York City was Union Square Cafe. It was a hit almost from the day it opened. Jeffrey and I lived a block away so we would go whenever we could get a reservation. Everything on the menu is delicious, but I always had to order the mashed turnips with crispy shallots. I was deliriously happy when Danny and chef Michael Romano published this recipe in their wonderful Union Square Cafe Cookbook.

1½ cups light olive or vegetable oil
3 tablespoons unsalted butter
5 to 6 shallots, peeled and sliced into thin rings
2 large yellow turnips (rutabagas), about 4 pounds total
Kosher salt
1 cup whole milk
6 tablespoons (¾ stick) salted butter
½ teaspoon freshly ground black pepper

Heat the oil and unsalted butter in a saucepan over medium-low heat until it reaches 220 degrees. Reduce the heat to low, add the shallots, and cook until they are a rich golden brown, 30 to 40 minutes. The temperature should stay below 260 degrees. Stir the shallots occasionally to make sure they brown evenly. Remove them from the oil with a slotted spoon, drain well, and spread out to cool on paper towels. Once they have dried and crisped, they can be stored at room temperature, covered, for several days.

Peel the turnips to remove the waxy skins and cut them into generous 1-inch chunks. Place them in a saucepan with water to cover and 1 teaspoon of salt. Bring to boil and simmer, covered, until easily pierced by a paring knife, about 35 minutes. Drain.

In a separate saucepan, heat the milk and salted butter over low heat until the butter has melted and the milk just begins to simmer.

Puree the turnips in several batches in a food processor fitted with the steel blade. With the motor running, add the melted butter and milk in a steady stream. The turnips should be smooth.

Return the puree to the saucepan, season with 1 teaspoon salt and the pepper, and reheat, stirring, over medium heat. Serve piping hot, sprinkled generously with crispy shallots.

Cut off the ends of the turnips and then peel them. When cutting hard root vegetables, be careful with the knife!

Yellow turnips, or rutabagas, are those large waxy root vegetables available in autumn and winter.

Danny calls for salted butter to finish; or you could use unsalted butter and add a little salt to finish.

STRING BEANS WITH SHALLOTS

Serves 6

French string beans are the slender ones you are most likely to find in specialty markets, but you can also make this with regular string beans. This recipe can be prepared almost entirely in advance. After the string beans are blanched, all you have to do is sauté the shallots in butter and toss the beans in the pan until they're warm.

> 1 pound French string beans (haricots verts), ends removed
> Kosher salt
> 2 tablespoons unsalted butter
> 1 tablespoon good olive oil
> 3 large shallots, large-diced
> ½ teaspoon freshly ground black pepper

Blanch the string beans in a large pot of boiling salted water for 1½ minutes only. Drain immediately and immerse in a bowl of ice water.

Heat the butter and oil in a very large sauté pan (12-inch diameter) or large pot and sauté the shallots on medium heat for 5 to 10 minutes, tossing occasionally, until lightly browned. Drain the string beans and add to the shallots with ½ teaspoon salt and the pepper, tossing well. Heat only until the beans are hot.

If you're using regular string beans, blanch them for about 3 minutes, until they're crisp-tender.

PROVENÇAL TOMATOES

Serves 8

When I was first married, I studied Julia Childs's Mastering the Art of French Cooking *as if it were the Bible. Once, we had very important guests coming for dinner, and I cooked Julia's roast leg of lamb and stuffed Provençal tomatoes three times that week to make sure the dinner would be perfect. By the time the appointed day arrived, my husband was groaning at the thought of lamb, but he rehearsed saying "This is delicious!" as though he'd never tasted it before. These tomatoes are very similar to that classic recipe.*

6 ripe tomatoes (2 ½ to 3 inches in diameter)
1 ½ cups fresh white bread crumbs (5 slices, crusts removed)
¼ cup minced scallions, white and green parts (2 scallions)
¼ cup minced fresh basil leaves
2 tablespoons minced fresh flat-leaf parsley
2 teaspoons minced garlic (2 cloves)
½ teaspoon minced fresh thyme leaves
Kosher salt
Freshly ground black pepper
½ cup grated Gruyère cheese
Good olive oil

Preheat the oven to 400 degrees.

Cut the cores from the tomatoes, removing as little as possible. Cut them in half crosswise and, with your fingers, remove the seeds and juice. Place the tomato halves in a baking dish.

In a bowl, combine the bread crumbs, scallions, basil, parsley, garlic, thyme, and 1 teaspoon salt. Sprinkle the tomato halves generously with salt and pepper. With your hands, fill the cavities and cover the tops of the tomatoes with the bread crumb mixture. Bake the tomatoes for 15 minutes, or until they're tender. Sprinkle with the cheese, drizzle with olive oil, and bake for 30 seconds more. Serve hot or at room temperature.

To make fresh bread crumbs, remove the crusts of Pepperidge Farm sandwich white bread or other fine-grained white bread. Cut the bread in cubes and pulse in a food processor until finely minced.

You can prepare the tomatoes and filling and refrigerate them. Bake just before serving.

MASHED POTATOES

Serves 6

While I was talking to the Women's Athletic Club in Chicago last year, one of the guests gave me a great idea for keeping mashed potatoes warm: put them in a bowl set over simmering water and they'll stay warm for at least half an hour. What a convenience! I now use this method for any pureed vegetable; just note that the longer the vegetable sits over hot water, the more liquid you'll need to add.

3 pounds white boiling potatoes, peeled and quartered
Kosher salt
¼ pound (1 stick) unsalted butter
½ to 1 cup half-and-half
½ cup sour cream
½ teaspoon freshly ground black pepper

Cook the potatoes in a large pot of boiling salted water for 15 to 20 minutes, until very tender. Meanwhile, heat the butter and half-and-half in a small saucepan.

Drain the potatoes. While still hot, place the potatoes in the bowl of an electric mixer fitted with the paddle attachment. With the mixer on low speed, slowly add the hot half-and-half mixture, the sour cream, 2 teaspoons salt, and the pepper. Mix until the potatoes are mashed but not completely smooth. Serve hot with gravy on the side.

If you plan to serve the mashed potatoes right away, just use less half-and-half. If you are keeping them hot for up to 30 minutes, use more.

HOMEMADE GRAVY

Makes 3 cups

At Barefoot Contessa we made thousands of quarts of gravy for people to heat up and serve for dinner. Instead of the chaos that happens when dinner is ready and you still have to make the gravy, why not give yourself a break and make the gravy the day before? If gravy just isn't gravy to you unless it's made with pan drippings, do what I do: when I make a roast, I save the pan drippings in the freezer for the next time I'm making gravy and then I add them to the sautéing onions and butter. It's so much easier! (Just be sure to label the drippings well.)

¼ pound (1 stick) unsalted butter
1½ cups chopped yellow onion (2 onions)
¼ cup all-purpose flour
1 teaspoon kosher salt
½ teaspoon freshly ground black pepper
2 cups chicken stock, preferably homemade (page 93), heated
1 tablespoon Cognac or brandy
1 tablespoon heavy cream (optional)

In a large (10- to 12-inch) sauté pan, cook the butter and onions on medium-low heat for 12 to 15 minutes, until the onions are lightly browned. Don't rush this step; it makes all the difference when the onions are well cooked.

Sprinkle the flour into the pan, whisk in, then add the salt and pepper. Cook for 2 to 3 minutes. Add the hot chicken stock and Cognac, and cook uncovered for 4 to 5 minutes, until thickened. Add the cream, if desired, and serve.

Gravy can be stored in the refrigerator for several days. Heat it slowly before serving.

Cognac is brandy from the Cognac region of France. Any good brandy will do.

You can substitute beef stock or pan drippings for the 2 cups of chicken stock.

ZUCCHINI WITH PARMESAN

Serves 6 to 8

Everyone who has a garden finds out that a few zucchini plants go a long way. So why am I still compelled to buy a whole flat of seedlings at the nursery every spring? I end up spending the rest of the summer finding new ways to cook zucchini. This recipe is my husband's favorite.

> 8 medium zucchini
> Good olive oil
> 2 large yellow onions cut in half and sliced ½ inch thick
> Kosher salt
> Freshly ground black pepper
> ½ cup freshly grated Parmesan cheese

Remove the ends of the zucchini and cut in half lengthwise. Slice the zucchini diagonally in ½-inch slices.

Heat 2 tablespoons of olive oil in a large (12-inch) sauté pan and add the onions. Cook for 10 minutes on medium-low heat, until they start to brown. Add half the zucchini, 1 teaspoon salt, and ¼ teaspoon pepper to the pan and cook, tossing occasionally, for 10 to 15 minutes, until just cooked through. Sprinkle with Parmesan and cook for 30 seconds more. Remove to a serving platter and repeat with the rest of the zucchini. Serve immediately.

If you cook too much zucchini in one pan, you end up steaming rather than sautéing it. I prefer to cook it in two batches.

SAUTÉED CARROTS

Serves 6

I'm always looking for ways to bring out the essential flavor of an ingredient. You don't want everything on your plate to shout at you; some things need to be more subtle for balance. These sautéed carrots are the essence of "carrot-ness." If you can find them, the ones with the tops still attached tend to be sweeter.

2 pounds carrots
1 teaspoon kosher salt
¼ teaspoon freshly ground black pepper
2 tablespoons unsalted butter
1½ tablespoons chopped fresh dill or flat-leaf parsley

Peel the carrots and cut them diagonally in ¼-inch slices. You should have about 6 cups of carrots. Place the carrots, ⅓ cup water, the salt, and pepper in a large (10- to 12-inch) sauté pan and bring to a boil. Cover the pan and cook over medium-low heat for 7 to 8 minutes, until the carrots are just cooked through. Add the butter and sauté for another minute, until the water evaporates and the carrots are coated with butter. Off the heat, toss with the dill or parsley. Sprinkle with salt and pepper and serve.

Carrots can be cut a day ahead and stored covered in water in the refrigerator. Drain well before using.

GARLIC SAUTÉED SPINACH

Serves 6

The bad news is that this needs to be made just before you sit down; the good news is that it only takes about 5 minutes. I prefer tender leaves of fresh baby spinach to the large bags of crinkled spinach you can find in the grocery store. Make this in the summer when baby spinach is available.

1½ pounds baby spinach leaves
2 tablespoons good olive oil
2 tablespoons chopped garlic (6 cloves)
2 teaspoons kosher salt
¾ teaspoon freshly ground black pepper
1 tablespoon unsalted butter
Lemon
Sea salt (optional)

Rinse the spinach well in cold water to make sure it's very clean. Spin it dry in a salad spinner, leaving just a little water clinging to the leaves.

In a very large pot or Dutch oven, heat the olive oil and sauté the garlic over medium heat for about 1 minute, but not until it's browned. Add all the spinach, the salt, and pepper to the pot, toss it with the garlic and oil, cover the pot, and cook it for 2 minutes. Uncover the pot, turn the heat on high, and cook the spinach for another minute, stirring with a wooden spoon, until all the spinach is wilted. Using a slotted spoon, lift the spinach to a serving bowl and top with the butter, a squeeze of lemon, and a sprinkling of sea or kosher salt. Serve hot.

Fresh spinach cooks down to nothing; don't be surprised at the volume of fresh spinach you need to serve six.

MASHED BUTTERNUT SQUASH

Serves 6

It's always exciting when a recipe evolves to the next level. One day I was making roasted butternut squash from The Barefoot Contessa Cookbook *and decided to try it as a puree—and it's even better! Serve this with a salty roasted vegetable like Brussels sprouts or Parmesan Roasted Asparagus (page 46) so you have contrasting flavors, colors, and textures.*

2 medium butternut squash (4 to 5 pounds total)
6 tablespoons (¾ stick) unsalted butter, melted
¼ cup light brown sugar, packed
1 ½ teaspoons kosher salt
½ teaspoon freshly ground black pepper
¼ cup half-and-half

Preheat the oven to 400 degrees.

Cut off and discard the ends of the butternut squash. Peel the squash, cut them in half lengthwise, and remove the seeds. Cut the squash into ¾-inch cubes and place them on a baking sheet. Add the melted butter, brown sugar, salt, and pepper. Toss all the ingredients together and spread in a single layer. Roast for 40 minutes, or until the squash is very tender. While roasting, turn the squash once with a spatula to be sure it cooks evenly. Don't let it brown.

In two batches, transfer the squash, the pan liquids, and half-and-half to the bowl of a food processor fitted with a steel blade. Pulse until the squash is coarsely pureed. It should have the consistency of mashed potatoes. To keep hot, place the puree in a bowl sitting over a pot of simmering water and stir. Season to taste and serve hot.

This can be made a few days in advance. Reheat it covered in the microwave or in a bowl over a pot of simmering water.

If the squash is too thick, thin it with milk, orange juice, or water.

SAGAPONACK CORN PUDDING

Serves 8

I find most corn puddings too bland, so I spent days trying to figure out how to make a version with the volume turned up. When my dear friend Frank Newbold requested this for Christmas dinner, I knew I had success. I think the basil and extra-sharp Cheddar give it good flavor without overpowering the delicate corn. If you can't get fresh corn, use frozen.

¼ pound (1 stick) unsalted butter
5 cups fresh corn kernels cut off the cob (6 to 8 ears)
1 cup chopped yellow onion (1 onion)
4 extra-large eggs
1 cup milk
1 cup half-and-half
½ cup yellow cornmeal
1 cup ricotta cheese
3 tablespoons chopped fresh basil leaves
1 tablespoon sugar
1 tablespoon kosher salt
¾ teaspoon freshly ground black pepper
¾ cup (6 ounces) grated extra-sharp Cheddar, plus extra to sprinkle on top

Preheat the oven to 375 degrees. Grease the inside of an 8- to 10-cup baking dish.

Melt the butter in a very large sauté pan and sauté the corn and onion over medium-high heat for 4 minutes. Cool slightly.

Whisk together the eggs, milk, and half-and-half in a large bowl. Slowly whisk in the cornmeal and then the ricotta. Add the basil, sugar, salt, and pepper. Add the cooked corn mixture and grated Cheddar, and then pour into the baking dish. Sprinkle the top with more grated Cheddar.

Place the dish in a larger pan and fill the pan halfway up the sides of the dish with hot tap water. Bake the pudding for 40 to 45 minutes, until the top begins to brown and a knife inserted in the center comes out clean. Serve warm.

WILD RICE PILAF

My friend the cookbook author Patricia Wells says that if you salt things as you cook, they taste well seasoned; if you salt them after you're done, they just taste salty. I think it's really smart advice, particularly when it comes to rice and pasta. This is a relatively expensive side dish but it's perfect for a special occasion, such as Sunday Rib Roast (page 76) or even for a simple roast chicken dinner.

> 3 tablespoons unsalted butter, divided
> ½ cup chopped yellow onion
> Kosher salt
> 2 cups pure wild rice (10 to 12 ounces)
> ¼ cup finely chopped scallions, white and green parts
>   (2 scallions)
> 1½ teaspoons freshly ground black pepper

Melt 2 tablespoons of the butter in a medium saucepan, add the onion, and cook over low heat for 5 to 10 minutes, until translucent. Add 5 cups of water, 2 teaspoons of salt, and the wild rice. Bring to a boil, reduce the heat to very low, and simmer, covered, for 50 minutes to 1 hour, until the rice is tender. Drain well.

Place the drained rice in a bowl, add the remaining tablespoon of butter, the scallions, 1½ teaspoons salt, and the pepper. Taste for seasonings and serve hot.

ROSEMARY POLENTA

Serves 12 to 18

Recipes handed down from friend to friend are wonderful. This one started life with Mike Leppizzera from Mike's Kitchen in Cranston, Rhode Island, and made its way into George Germon and Johanne Killeen's wonderful book, Cucina Simpatica, *where I first discovered it. At Barefoot Contessa we made a few changes and added fresh rosemary. The good news is that the polenta can be made days in advance and then sautéed just before serving.*

¼ pound (1 stick) unsalted butter
¼ cup olive oil
1 tablespoon minced garlic (3 cloves)
1 teaspoon crushed red pepper flakes
1 teaspoon minced fresh rosemary leaves
½ teaspoon kosher salt
½ teaspoon freshly ground black pepper
3 cups chicken stock, preferably homemade (page 93)
2 cups half-and-half
2 cups milk
2 cups cornmeal
½ cup good grated Parmesan cheese
Flour, olive oil, and butter, for frying

Heat the butter and olive oil in a large saucepan. Add the garlic, red pepper flakes, rosemary, salt, and pepper and sauté for 1 minute. Add the chicken stock, half-and-half, and milk and bring to a boil. Remove from the heat and slowly sprinkle the cornmeal into the hot milk while stirring constantly with a whisk. Cook over low heat, stirring constantly, for a few minutes, until thickened and bubbly. Off the heat, stir in the Parmesan. Pour into a 9 × 13 × 2-inch pan, smooth the top, and refrigerate until firm and cold.

Cut the chilled polenta into 12 squares, as you would with brownies. Lift each one out with a spatula and cut diagonally into triangles. Dust each triangle lightly in flour. Heat 1 tablespoon olive oil and 1 tablespoon butter in a large sauté pan and cook the triangles in batches over medium heat for 3 to 5 minutes, turning once, until browned on the outside and heated inside. Add more butter and oil, as needed. Serve immediately.

For a vegetarian dinner, prepare the polenta with vegetable stock and serve one whole square per person. As a side dish, serve one triangle per person.

The exact measurement of the pan is not important. If the pan is a little smaller, the polenta will only be a little thicker.

Keep the polenta warm in a 250-degree oven while you sauté the rest of the triangles.

Summer Pudding, page 168

DESSERTS

RASPBERRY Cheesecake

FROZEN Key Lime Pie

Espresso ICE CREAM

ORANGE Pound Cake

Raspberry Orange TRIFLE

Rum Raisin RICE PUDDING

Stewed Berries & ICE CREAM

PUMPKIN BANANA Mousse Tart

FLAG Cake

DEEP-DISH Apple Pie

Coconut MACAROONS

LEMON Angel Food Cake

Chocolate MOUSSE

Summer Pudding
WITH RUM WHIPPED CREAM

Tiramisù

RASPBERRY CHEESECAKE

Serves 12 to 15

For me, this is the quintessential cheesecake. It's creamy but light with vanilla and lemon undertones. Amazingly, it doesn't crack in the middle like every other cheesecake I've ever made, so it looks great if you serve it alone. The fresh raspberries are so delicious on top, though, why would you want to?

FOR THE CRUST
1 ½ cups graham cracker crumbs (10 crackers)
1 tablespoon sugar
6 tablespoons (¾ stick) unsalted butter, melted

FOR THE FILLING
2 ½ pounds cream cheese, at room temperature
1 ½ cups sugar
5 whole extra-large eggs, at room temperature
2 extra-large egg yolks, at room temperature
¼ cup sour cream
1 tablespoon grated lemon zest (2 lemons)
1 ½ teaspoons pure vanilla extract

FOR THE TOPPING (OPTIONAL)
1 cup red jelly (not jam) such as currant, raspberry, or strawberry
3 half-pints fresh raspberries

Preheat the oven to 350 degrees.

To make the crust, combine the graham crackers, sugar, and melted butter until moistened. Pour into a 9-inch springform pan. With your hands, press the crumbs into the bottom of the pan and about 1 inch up the sides. Bake for 8 minutes. Cool to room temperature.

Raise the oven temperature to 450 degrees.

To make the filling, cream the cream cheese and sugar in the bowl of an electric mixer fitted with a paddle attachment on medium-high speed until light and fluffy, about 5 minutes. Reduce the speed of the mixer to medium and add the eggs and egg yolks, two at a time, mixing well. Scrape down the bowl

and beater as necessary. With the mixer on low, add the sour cream, lemon zest, and vanilla. Mix thoroughly and pour into the cooled crust.

Bake for 15 minutes. Turn the oven temperature down to 225 degrees and bake for another 1 hour and 15 minutes. Turn the oven off and open the door wide. The cake will not be completely set in the center. Allow the cake to sit in the oven with the door open for 30 minutes. Take the cake out of the oven and allow it to sit at room temperature for another 2 to 3 hours, until completely cooled. Wrap and refrigerate overnight.

Remove the cake from the springform pan by carefully running a hot knife around the outside of the cake. Leave the cake on the bottom of the springform pan for serving.

If you make the topping, melt the jelly in a small pan over low heat. In a bowl, toss the raspberries and the warm jelly gently until well mixed. Arrange the berries on top of the cake. Refrigerate until ready to serve.

Measure your springform pan. The bottom of mine measures 9 inches, but it says 9½.

I put the springform pan on a sheet pan before putting it in the oven to catch any leaks.

FROZEN KEY LIME PIE

Serves 8

In Florida, Key lime pie is made with the juice of those small, tart Key limes. Since they're hard to find anywhere else, I made this pie in the same style but with regular fresh limes. Make it days in advance (it lasts for months in the freezer) so you can be relaxed for your own party.

FOR THE CRUST
1½ cups graham cracker crumbs (10 crackers)
¼ cup sugar
6 tablespoons (¾ stick) unsalted butter, melted

FOR THE FILLING
6 extra-large egg yolks, at room temperature
¼ cup sugar
1 14-ounce can sweetened condensed milk
2 tablespoons grated lime zest
¾ cup freshly squeezed lime juice (4 to 5 limes)

FOR THE DECORATION
1 cup (½ pint) cold heavy cream
¼ cup sugar
¼ teaspoon pure vanilla extract
Thin lime wedges

Preheat the oven to 350 degrees.

For the crust, combine the graham cracker crumbs, sugar, and butter in a bowl. Press into a 9-inch pie pan, making sure the sides and the bottom are an even thickness. Bake for 10 minutes. Allow to cool completely.

For the filling, beat the egg yolks and sugar on high speed in the bowl of an electric mixer fitted with a paddle attachment for 5 minutes, until thick. With the mixer on medium speed, add the condensed milk, lime zest, and lime juice. Pour into the baked pie shell and freeze.

For the decoration, beat the heavy cream on high speed in the bowl of an electric mixer fitted with the whisk attachment until soft peaks form. Add the sugar and vanilla and beat until firm. Spoon or pipe decoratively onto the pie and decorate with lime. Freeze for several hours or overnight.

If you have concerns about raw eggs, combine the yolks with $1/2$ cup of the lime juice used in the recipe in a double boiler. Whisk constantly over medium heat until the mixture reaches 140 degrees. Use in place of the raw egg yolks, remembering to add the remaining $1/4$ cup of lime juice to the filling mixture along with the condensed milk and zest.

Cold limes are easier to zest but room-temperature limes give up more juice.

ESPRESSO ICE CREAM

Makes 1 quart

One day at Barefoot Contessa I drank an iced coffee while nibbling a few chocolate-covered espresso beans and realized the flavors would be terrific together in a dessert. For this ice cream, I use ground espresso beans. If you make it with regular, rather than decaffeinated, espresso, you hardly need to serve coffee with dinner!

3 cups half-and-half
6 extra-large egg yolks
⅔ cup sugar
Pinch of salt
2½ tablespoons ground espresso coffee beans, decaffeinated or regular
1 tablespoon Kahlúa liqueur
1 teaspoon pure vanilla extract
4 ounces (½ cup) chocolate-covered espresso beans, chopped

Heat the half-and-half until it forms bubbles around the edge of the pan and steam starts to rise. Meanwhile, in the bowl of an electric mixer fitted with the paddle attachment, beat the egg yolks, sugar, and salt until mixed. Slowly add the hot half-and-half until combined. Wipe out the pan and pour the mixture back into the clean pan. Cook over medium-low heat, stirring constantly with a wooden spoon, for 5 to 10 minutes, until it's thickened and the cream coats the back of the spoon. Pour the cream through a fine-meshed sieve into a bowl. Add the ground espresso beans, Kahlúa, and vanilla and refrigerate until completely chilled.

Pour the espresso cream into an ice-cream freezer and freeze according to the manufacturer's directions. Mix in the chopped espresso beans, spoon into a container, and allow to freeze for a few hours. Soften slightly before serving.

Be sure you have finely ground espresso beans, not instant espresso.

I love the espresso beans that are covered in chocolate, but you can also use the chocolate candy that looks like espresso beans.

ORANGE POUND CAKE

Makes 2 loaves

This cake is a variation on the ever-popular Lemon Cake in Barefoot Contessa Parties! *It's great on its own with a cup of tea, or as the basis for a summer trifle with orange pastry cream and fresh raspberries. Since the recipe makes two loaves, you can serve one now and freeze the second one for another day. If you're making the trifle or freezing the loaf, omit the glaze.*

½ pound (2 sticks) unsalted butter, at room temperature
2½ cups granulated sugar, divided
4 extra-large eggs, at room temperature
⅓ cup grated orange zest (6 oranges)
3 cups all-purpose flour
½ teaspoon baking powder
½ teaspoon baking soda
1 teaspoon kosher salt
¾ cup freshly squeezed orange juice, divided
¾ cup buttermilk, at room temperature
1 teaspoon pure vanilla extract

TO GLAZE ONE LOAF (OPTIONAL)
1 cup confectioners' sugar, sifted
1½ tablespoons freshly squeezed orange juice

Heat the oven to 350 degrees. Grease and flour two 8½ × 4½ × 2½-inch loaf pans. Line the bottoms with parchment paper.

Cream the butter and 2 cups of the granulated sugar in the bowl of an electric mixer fitted with the paddle attachment for about 5 minutes, or until light and fluffy. With the mixer on medium speed, beat in the eggs, one at a time, and the orange zest.

In a large bowl, sift together the flour, baking powder, baking soda, and salt. In another bowl, combine ¼ cup of the orange juice, the buttermilk, and vanilla. Add the flour and buttermilk mixtures alternately to the batter, beginning and ending with the flour. Divide the batter evenly between the pans, smooth the tops, and bake for 45 minutes to 1 hour, until a cake tester comes out clean.

While the cakes bake, cook the remaining ½ cup of granulated sugar with the remaining ½ cup orange juice in a small saucepan over low heat until the sugar dissolves. When the cakes are done, let them cool for 10 minutes. Take them out of the pans and place them on a baking rack set over a tray. Spoon the orange syrup over the cakes and allow the cakes to cool completely.

To glaze, combine the confectioners' sugar and orange juice in a bowl, mixing with a wire whisk until smooth. Add a few more drops of juice, if necessary, to make it pour easily. Pour over the top of one cake and allow the glaze to dry. Wrap well, and store in the refrigerator.

RASPBERRY ORANGE TRIFLE

Serves 6 to 8

Trifle is a classic English dish that was a frugal cook's idea for using leftover cake. It's traditionally served at Christmastime but I thought it would be fun to have a summer trifle with orange pound cake and fresh raspberries. You should feel free to use your imagination with whatever you have in the house, or just buy plain pound cake from the store and add raspberry jam, raspberries, and whipped cream. Who would hate that?

1 Orange Pound Cake (page 142), unglazed
1 cup good raspberry jam
2 half-pints fresh raspberries
Orange Cream (page 146)
1 cup (½ pint) cold heavy cream
2 tablespoons sugar
½ teaspoon pure vanilla extract

Cut the pound cake into nine ¾-inch slices and spread each slice on one side with raspberry jam, using all the jam. Set aside.

Place a layer of cake, jam side up, in the bottom of a 2½- to 3-quart glass serving bowl, cutting the pieces to fit. Top with a layer of raspberries and orange cream. Repeat the layers of cake, raspberries, and orange cream, ending with a third layer of cake jam side down and raspberries.

Whip the cream in the bowl of an electric mixer fitted with the whisk attachment. When it starts to thicken, add the sugar and vanilla and continue to whip until it forms stiff peaks. Decorate the trifle with whipped cream. The trifle can sit for a while at room temperature.

The cake and orange cream can be made several days in advance. Whip the cream and assemble the dessert before dinner.

Orange Cream

Makes 2 cups

1 ½ cups milk
1 teaspoon grated orange zest (1 orange)
5 extra-large egg yolks, at room temperature
½ cup sugar
2 tablespoons sifted cornstarch
½ teaspoon pure vanilla extract
½ teaspoon Grand Marnier liqueur
1 tablespoon unsalted butter
1 tablespoon heavy cream

Combine the milk and orange zest in a medium stainless-steel saucepan over medium heat and bring almost to a boil. Remove from the heat.

Beat the egg yolks and sugar on medium-high speed in the bowl of an electric mixer fitted with the paddle attachment until pale and thick, about 5 minutes. With the mixer on low speed, sprinkle on the cornstarch. Beat on medium-low speed until combined, scraping down the bowl with a rubber spatula.

With the mixer on low speed, slowly pour the hot milk mixture into the egg mixture. Pour the mixture back into the pan. Cook over low heat, stirring constantly, until the mixture thickens, 5 to 7 minutes. (Pay attention because it will thicken and then quickly become orange scrambled eggs!)

Immediately, pour the mixture through a fine sieve into a large bowl. Stir in the vanilla, Grand Marnier, butter, and heavy cream. Place plastic wrap directly on the custard and refrigerate until cold.

I use a wooden spoon to stir the custard on the stove and then beat it with a whisk as soon as it thickens. The custard will coat a metal spoon when it's done.

RUM RAISIN RICE PUDDING

Serves 6 to 8

Men, especially, love nursery desserts, but rice pudding can be really boring. For this recipe, don't think rice pudding, think rum raisin ice cream, because it borrows its flavor from my favorite Häagen-Dazs ice cream.

¾ cup raisins
2 tablespoons dark rum
¾ cup white basmati rice
½ teaspoon kosher salt
5 cups half-and-half, divided
½ cup sugar
1 extra-large egg, beaten
1½ teaspoons pure vanilla extract

In a small bowl, combine the raisins and rum. Set aside.

Combine the rice and salt with 1½ cups water in a medium heavy-bottomed stainless steel saucepan. Bring it to a boil, stir once, and simmer, covered, on the lowest heat for 8 to 9 minutes, until most of the water is absorbed. (If your stove is very hot, pull the pan halfway off the burner.)

Stir in 4 cups of half-and-half and sugar and bring to a boil. Simmer uncovered for 25 minutes, until the rice is very soft. Stir often, particularly toward the end. Slowly stir in the beaten egg and continue to cook for 1 minute. Off the heat, add the remaining cup of half-and-half, the vanilla, and the raisins with any remaining rum. Stir well. Pour into a bowl, and place a piece of plastic wrap directly on top of the pudding to prevent a skin from forming. Serve warm or chilled.

I use Texmati organic basmati rice.

If the pudding becomes too thick after it's refrigerated, stir in more half-and-half.

STEWED BERRIES
& ICE CREAM

Serves 6

I love accidents. I was testing the recipe for summer pudding when I decided that the stewed berries, which were an ingredient in the pudding, were also delicious alone. Since they only take a few minutes to make, this is a great last-minute dessert. Framboise, a raspberry liqueur, gives it extra zing.

3 half-pints fresh raspberries, divided
2 half-pints fresh blueberries
1 ½ cups sugar
2 tablespoons framboise (raspberry brandy), optional
2 pints good vanilla ice cream

Combine 2 half-pints of raspberries, all the blueberries, sugar, and ¾ cup water in a saucepan and bring to a boil. Lower the heat and cook uncovered over medium-low heat, stirring occasionally, for 10 to 12 minutes. The juice will become a syrup and the berries will be slightly cooked. Off the heat, stir in the remaining half-pint of raspberries and the framboise, if desired. Set aside until warmed through.

Place about ¾ cup of warm berries in each bowl and top with a scoop of ice cream.

PUMPKIN BANANA MOUSSE TART

Serves 10

I wrote this recipe for my entertaining series for O, Oprah's magazine. It was inspired by a pumpkin mousse that my mother had made for years for Thanksgiving. It's lighter and much more flavorful than that cloying old pumpkin pie. People really do go nuts for it.

FOR THE CRUST
2 cups graham cracker crumbs (14 crackers)
1/3 cup sugar
1/4 teaspoon ground cinnamon
1/4 pound (1 stick) unsalted butter, melted

FOR THE FILLING
1/2 cup half-and-half
1 15-ounce can pumpkin puree
1 cup light brown sugar, lightly packed
3/4 teaspoon kosher salt
1/2 teaspoon ground cinnamon
1/4 teaspoon ground nutmeg
3 extra-large egg yolks
1 package (2 teaspoons) unflavored gelatin
1 ripe banana, finely mashed
1/2 teaspoon grated orange zest
1/2 cup cold heavy cream
2 tablespoons sugar

FOR THE DECORATION
1 cup (1/2 pint) cold heavy cream
1/4 cup sugar
1/4 teaspoon pure vanilla extract
Orange zest (optional)

Preheat the oven to 350 degrees.

Combine the graham cracker crumbs, sugar, cinnamon, and melted butter in a bowl and mix well. Pour into an 11-inch tart pan with a removable bottom and press evenly into the sides and then the bottom. Bake for 10 minutes and then cool to room temperature.

For the filling, heat the half-and-half, pumpkin, brown sugar, salt, cinnamon, and nutmeg in a heat-proof bowl set over a pan of simmering water until hot, about 5 minutes. Whisk the egg yolks in another bowl, stir some of the hot pumpkin into the egg yolks to heat them, then pour the egg-pumpkin mixture back into the double boiler and stir well. Heat the mixture over the simmering water for another 4 to 5 minutes, until it begins to thicken, stirring constantly. You don't want the eggs to scramble. Remove from the heat.

Dissolve the gelatin in ¼ cup cold water. Add the dissolved gelatin, banana, and orange zest to the pumpkin mixture and mix well. Set aside to cool.

Whip the heavy cream in the bowl of an electric mixer fitted with a whisk attachment until soft peaks form. Add the sugar and continue to whisk until you have firm peaks. Carefully fold the whipped cream into the pumpkin mixture and pour it into the cooled tart shell. Chill for 2 hours or overnight.

For the decoration, whip the heavy cream in the bowl of an electric mixer fitted with the whisk attachment until soft peaks form. Add the sugar and vanilla and continue to whisk until you have firm peaks. Pipe or spoon the whipped cream decoratively on the tart and sprinkle, if desired, with orange zest. Serve chilled.

This tart can be made a day or two ahead and kept refrigerated. Decorate it with whipped cream an hour or two before serving.

FLAG CAKE

Serves 20 to 24

This was definitely the most-requested recipe from my column in Martha Stewart Living *magazine. It's a really big cake and you certainly can cut it in half if you like, but it's so dramatic to serve, why not make the whole thing? I frost the cake and let my guests do the decorating. Everyone gets a piece to take home.*

18 tablespoons (2 ¼ sticks) unsalted butter, at room
  temperature
3 cups sugar
6 extra-large eggs, at room temperature
1 cup sour cream, at room temperature
1 ½ teaspoons pure vanilla extract
3 cups all-purpose flour
⅓ cup cornstarch
1 teaspoon kosher salt
1 teaspoon baking soda

FOR THE ICING
1 pound (4 sticks) unsalted butter, at room temperature
1 ½ pounds cream cheese, at room temperature
1 pound confectioners' sugar, sifted
1 ½ teaspoons pure vanilla extract

TO ASSEMBLE
2 half-pints blueberries
3 half-pints raspberries

Heat the oven to 350 degrees. Butter and flour an 18 × 12 × 1½-inch sheet pan.

Cream the butter and sugar in the bowl of an electric mixer fitted with the paddle attachment on high speed, until light and fluffy. On medium speed, add the eggs, 2 at a time, then add the sour cream and vanilla. Scrape down the sides and stir until smooth.

Sift together the flour, cornstarch, salt, and baking soda in a bowl. With the mixer on low speed, add the flour mixture to the butter mixture until just combined. Pour into the prepared pan. Smooth the top with a spatula. Bake in the center of the oven for 20 to 30 minutes, until a toothpick comes out clean. Cool to room temperature.

For the icing, combine the butter, cream cheese, sugar, and vanilla in the bowl of an electric mixer fitted with the paddle attachment, mixing just until smooth.

Spread three fourths of the icing on the top of the cooled sheet cake. Outline the flag on the top of the cake with a toothpick. Fill the upper left corner with blueberries. Place 2 rows of raspberries across the top of the cake like a red stripe. Put the remaining icing in a pastry bag fitted with a star tip and pipe two rows of white stripes below the raspberries. Alternate rows of raspberries and icing until the flag is completed. Pipe stars on top of the blueberries.

I serve this cake right in the pan. If you want to turn it out onto a board, use parchment paper when you grease and flour the pan.

DEEP-DISH APPLE PIE

Makes one 10-inch pie

Apple pie has always been a problem for me. The apples either come out too hard or taste like applesauce. Some pies are overwhelmed with cinnamon or allspice when I just want the spices to bring out the "appleness" of the filling. I made pies for a week (my friends were beginning to groan) until I arrived at what I think is the quintessential apple pie. I hope you agree.

4 pounds Granny Smith apples, peeled, quartered, and cored
Zest of 1 lemon
Zest of 1 orange
2 tablespoons freshly squeezed lemon juice
1 tablespoon freshly squeezed orange juice
1/2 cup sugar, plus 1 teaspoon to sprinkle on top
1/4 cup all-purpose flour
1 teaspoon kosher salt
3/4 teaspoon ground cinnamon
1/2 teaspoon ground nutmeg
1/8 teaspoon ground allspice
Perfect Pie Crust (recipe follows)
1 egg beaten with 1 tablespoon water for egg wash

Preheat the oven to 400 degrees.

Cut each apple quarter in thirds crosswise and combine in a bowl with the zests, juices, sugar, flour, salt, cinnamon, nutmeg, and allspice.

Roll out half the pie dough and drape it over the pie pan to extend about 1/2 inch over the rim. Don't stretch the dough; if it's too small, just put it back on the board and re-roll it.

Fill the pie with the apple mixture. Brush the edge of the bottom pie crust with the egg wash so the top crust will adhere. Top with the second crust and trim the edges to about 1 inch over the rim. Tuck the edge of the top crust under the edge of the bottom crust and crimp the two together with your fingers or a fork. Brush the entire top crust with the egg wash, sprinkle with 1 teaspoon sugar, and cut four or five slits.

Place the pie on a sheet pan and bake for 1 to 1 1/4 hours, or until the crust is browned and the juices begin to bubble out. Serve warm.

Perfect Pie Crust

Makes two 10-inch crusts

Most people find making pie crust daunting. There are a few secrets that will change all that. First, the butter, shortening, and water must all be very cold. Second, let the dough sit in the refrigerator (bakers call it "relaxing" the dough) for 30 minutes before rolling, and finally, don't stretch the dough when you're placing it into the pan. Follow these tips and you'll have delicious, flaky pie crust every time.

12 tablespoons (1 ½ sticks) very cold unsalted butter
3 cups all-purpose flour
1 teaspoon kosher salt
1 tablespoon sugar
⅓ cup very cold vegetable shortening
6 to 8 tablespoons (about ½ cup) ice water

Dice the butter and return it to the refrigerator while you prepare the flour mixture. Place the flour, salt, and sugar in the bowl of a food processor fitted with a steel blade and pulse a few times to mix. Add the butter and shortening. Pulse 8 to 12 times, until the butter is the size of peas. With the machine running, pour the ice water down the feed tube and pulse the machine until the dough begins to form a ball. Dump out on a floured board and roll into a ball. Wrap in plastic wrap and refrigerate for 30 minutes.

Cut the dough in half. Roll each piece on a well-floured board into a circle, rolling from the center to the edge, turning and flouring the dough to make sure it doesn't stick to the board. Fold the dough in half, place in a pie pan, and unfold to fit the pan. Repeat with the top crust.

I prefer Crisco shortening. Since I use it only for pie crusts, I store it in the refrigerator so it's always cold.

COCONUT MACAROONS

Makes 20 to 22 cookies

So many people have asked me for this recipe! They're traditional for Passover because they don't have any flour, but I think they're wonderful any time of the year. They're definitely one of the best-selling cookies at Barefoot Contessa, and they're incredibly easy to make.

14 ounces sweetened shredded coconut
14 ounces sweetened condensed milk
1 teaspoon pure vanilla extract
2 extra-large egg whites, at room temperature
¼ teaspoon kosher salt

Preheat the oven to 325 degrees.

Combine the coconut, condensed milk, and vanilla in a large bowl. Whip the egg whites and salt on high speed in the bowl of an electric mixer fitted with the whisk attachment until they make medium-firm peaks. Carefully fold the egg whites into the coconut mixture.

Drop the batter onto sheet pans lined with parchment paper using either a 1¾-inch diameter ice cream scoop, or two teaspoons. Bake for 25 to 30 minutes, until golden brown. Cool and serve.

Sweetened coconut is sometimes called "flaked coconut."

These cookies will stay fresh for a few days if they're wrapped well and left at room temperature.

LEMON ANGEL FOOD CAKE

Serves 8

Angel food cake usually tastes like cotton candy to me, but this one has substance and flavor. It comes from my friend Laura Donnelly, whose extraordinary family has been in East Hampton since the 1920s. She is now the wonderful pastry chef at the Laundry Restaurant in East Hampton, where I've enjoyed many delicious dinners. Serve this plain, with sweetened fruit, or drizzled with ½ cup of confectioners' sugar mixed with 1 tablespoon of fresh lemon juice.

2 cups sifted superfine sugar, divided
1 ⅓ cups sifted cake flour (not self-rising)
1 ½ cups egg whites, at room temperature
   (10 to 12 eggs)
¾ teaspoon kosher salt
1 ½ teaspoons cream of tartar
¾ teaspoon pure vanilla extract
1 ½ teaspoons grated lemon zest (2 lemons)

Preheat the oven to 350 degrees.

Combine ½ cup of sugar with the flour and sift together 4 times. Set aside.

Place the egg whites, salt, and cream of tartar in the bowl of an electric mixer fitted with the whisk attachment and beat on high speed until the eggs make medium-firm peaks, about 1 minute. With the mixer on medium speed, add the remaining 1 ½ cups of sugar by sprinkling it over the beaten egg whites. Whisk for a few minutes until thick and shiny. Whisk in the vanilla and lemon zest and continue to whisk until very thick, about 1 more minute. Sift about one fourth of the flour mixture over the egg whites and fold it into the batter with a rubber spatula. Continue adding the flour by fourths by sifting and folding until it's all incorporated.

Pour the batter into an ungreased 10-inch tube pan, smooth the top, and bake it for 35 to 40 minutes, until it springs back to the touch. Remove the cake from the oven and invert the pan on a cooling rack until cool.

To store, wrap well and do not refrigerate.

CHOCOLATE MOUSSE

Serves 8

I have a weakness for French food. Not the fancy, "pinkies up" kind of French food with rich sauces; rather, I love basic bistro-style food you can find in so many neighborhood restaurants that still exist in Paris. Chicken in wine with a crusty French bread and chocolate mousse for dessert is my idea of a great meal. But I find this mousse goes equally well with very American oven-fried chicken (page 81).

1 cup semisweet chocolate chips
1 ounce unsweetened chocolate, chopped
¼ cup freshly brewed coffee
1 teaspoon instant coffee powder
¼ cup Grand Marnier liqueur
1 tablespoon Armagnac, Cognac, or brandy
1 teaspoon pure vanilla extract
12 tablespoons (1½ sticks) unsalted butter, diced, at room temperature
8 extra-large eggs, separated, at room temperature
½ cup sugar plus 2 tablespoons, divided
Kosher salt
½ cup cold heavy cream
Sweetened whipped cream, for decoration

In a heat-proof bowl set over a pan of simmering water, melt the two chocolates, coffee, coffee powder, Grand Marnier, Armagnac, and vanilla extract. Cool to room temperature. Beat in the softened butter.

Meanwhile, place the egg yolks and the ½ cup of sugar in the bowl of an electric mixer fitted with the paddle attachment. Beat on high speed for about 5 minutes, until pale yellow; when you lift the beater, the mixture will fall back on itself in a ribbon. With the mixer on low speed, blend in the chocolate mixture. Transfer to a larger mixing bowl.

Measure 1 cup of egg whites and freeze or discard the rest. Combine the cup of egg whites with a pinch of salt and 1 tablespoon of the remaining sugar in the bowl of an electric mixer fitted with the whisk attachment. Whisk on

high speed until stiff but not dry. Mix half of the egg whites into the choco-late mixture; then fold the rest in carefully with a rubber spatula.

In the same bowl of the electric mixer fitted with the whisk attachment, whisk the heavy cream and the remaining 1 tablespoon of sugar until firm. Carefully fold the whipped cream into the chocolate mixture. Pour the mousse into a 2-quart serving dish. Cover with plastic wrap and chill for a few hours or overnight and up to a week.

Decorate with sweetened whipped cream just before serving.

It is very important that the butter come completely to room temperature.

It's easier to separate cold eggs, but egg whites at room temperature whip better.

SUMMER PUDDING
WITH RUM WHIPPED CREAM

Serves 8

I've always found summer pudding a bit bland; it's an old-fashioned English dessert that was probably devised as a way to use up leftover bread and berries. I decided to make one with brioche and found it was really delicious. A big dollop of rum whipped cream doesn't hurt the flavor, either.

      1 pint fresh strawberries, hulled and sliced
      1 ½ cups sugar
      3 half-pints fresh raspberries, divided
      2 half-pints fresh blueberries
      2 tablespoons framboise (raspberry brandy)
      1 loaf brioche or egg bread (1 to 1 ½ pounds)

Combine the strawberries, sugar, and ¼ cup of water in a large saucepan and cook uncovered over medium-low heat for 5 minutes. Add 2 cups of the raspberries and all the blueberries and cook, stirring occasionally, until the mixture reaches a simmer, and simmer for a minute. Off the heat, stir in the remaining raspberries and the framboise.

Slice the bread in ½-inch-thick slices and remove the crusts. In the bottom of a 7 ½-inch round by 3-inch high soufflé or baking dish, ladle about ½ cup of the cooked berry mixture. Arrange slices of bread in a pattern (this will become the top when it's unmolded) and then add more berry mixture to saturate. Continue adding bread, cutting it to fit the mold, and berries. Finish with bread and cooked berries, using all of the fruit and syrup.

Place a sheet of plastic wrap loosely over the pudding. Find a plate approximately the same diameter as the inside of the mold and place it on top. Weight the mold with a heavy can and refrigerate. Remove the weight after 6 to 8 hours. Cover the pudding with plastic wrap and refrigerate overnight.

Just before serving, run a knife around the outside of the pudding and unmold it upside down onto a serving plate. Serve in wedges with rum whipped cream.

Summer pudding can be made a day ahead.

Rum Whipped Cream

Serves 8

Traditionally, whipped cream is flavored with sugar and vanilla, but I like to experiment with other flavors, like rum or cassis. Rum whipped cream is also the perfect accompaniment to Pumpkin Banana Mousse Tart (page 151)

I cup (½ pint) cold heavy cream
3 tablespoons sugar
½ teaspoon pure vanilla extract
I tablespoon dark rum

Whip the cream in the bowl of an electric mixer fitted with the whisk attachment. When it starts to thicken, add the sugar, vanilla, and rum. Continue to whip until it forms stiff peaks. Serve cold.

Cream that is not ultra-pasteurized will whip better.

TIRAMISÙ

Serves 8

Tiramisù was to the 1990s what Pasta Pesto was to the '80s—it was done, done, and overdone. Now that it's not so pervasive, I dragged out my old recipe and rediscovered a dessert that's delicious, can be made in advance, and requires no cooking! Any sweet chocolate can be shaved on top.

> 6 extra-large egg yolks, at room temperature
> ¼ cup sugar
> ½ cup good dark rum, divided
> 1½ cups brewed espresso, divided
> 16 to 17 ounces mascarpone cheese
> 30 Italian ladyfingers, or *savoiardi*
> Bittersweet chocolate, shaved or grated
> Confectioners' sugar (optional)

Whisk the egg yolks and sugar in the bowl of an electric mixer fitted with the whisk attachment on high speed for 5 minutes, until very thick and light yellow. Lower the speed to medium and add ¼ cup of rum, ¼ cup of espresso, and the mascarpone. Whisk until smooth.

Combine the remaining ¼ cup rum and 1¼ cups espresso in a shallow bowl. Dip one side of each ladyfinger in the espresso-rum mixture and line the bottom of a 9 × 12 × 2-inch dish. Pour half the espresso cream mixture evenly on top. Dip one side of the remaining ladyfingers in the espresso-rum mixture and place them in a second layer in the dish. Pour the rest of the espresso cream over the top. Smooth the top and cover with plastic wrap. Refrigerate overnight.

Before serving, sprinkle the top with shaved chocolate and dust lightly with confectioners' sugar, if desired.

To make espresso for this recipe in your electric drip coffee maker, use ⅓ cup of ground espresso and enough water for 4 cups of coffee.

Mascarpone is like an Italian cream cheese. If you can't find it in the grocery, try an Italian specialty store.

To shave chocolate, use a vegetable peeler on a bar of chocolate.

BREAKFAST

BLUEBERRY Coffee Cake Muffins

Banana Sour Cream PANCAKES

SLOW-COOKED Scrambled Eggs
THREE WAYS

Potato Basil FRITTATA

Smoked Salmon FRITTATA

CHALLAH French Toast

Hashed Browns

Bagels WITH FLAVORED CREAM CHEESE

CHIVE Biscuits

Fresh Fruit WITH
HONEY VANILLA YOGURT

BLUEBERRY COFFEE CAKE MUFFINS

Makes 16 muffins

There were days at Barefoot Contessa in Westhampton Beach when we would bake 2,000 muffins on a Saturday morning and they would all be gone by 9:30 A.M. As bakers came out of the kitchen with more muffins, people would try to grab them off the trays. I guess there's not much that's as appealing as a freshly baked muffin!

12 tablespoons (1½ sticks) unsalted butter, at room temperature
1½ cups sugar
3 extra-large eggs, at room temperature
1½ teaspoons pure vanilla extract
8 ounces (about 1 cup) sour cream
¼ cup milk
2½ cups all-purpose flour
2 teaspoons baking powder
½ teaspoon baking soda
½ teaspoon kosher salt
2 half-pints fresh blueberries, picked through for stems

Preheat the oven to 350 degrees. Place 16 paper liners in muffin pans.

In the bowl of an electric mixer fitted with the paddle attachment, cream the butter and sugar until light and fluffy, about 5 minutes. With the mixer on low speed, add the eggs one at a time, then add the vanilla, sour cream, and milk. In a separate bowl, sift together the flour, baking powder, baking soda, and salt. With the mixer on low speed add the flour mixture to the batter and beat until just mixed. Fold in the blueberries with a spatula and be sure the batter is completely mixed.

Scoop the batter into the prepared muffin pans, filling each cup just over the top, and bake for 25 to 30 minutes, until the muffins are lightly browned on top and a cake tester comes out clean.

The bakers at Barefoot Contessa use an ice-cream scoop to measure the batter so that every muffin comes out the same size.

Greasing the tops of the pans makes it easier to take the muffins out.

BANANA SOUR CREAM PANCAKES

Makes 12 pancakes

I spent a full weekend testing pancake recipes but they all tasted pretty much the same to me: good, but not exciting. Finally, I made these with sour cream, bananas, and vanilla and—served with bananas and maple syrup—they were a hit. My husband, Jeffrey, who was my taste tester, loved them but he had to take a long nap that afternoon!

1 ½ cups all-purpose flour
3 tablespoons sugar
2 teaspoons baking powder
1 ½ teaspoons kosher salt
½ cup sour cream
¾ cup plus 1 tablespoon milk
2 extra-large eggs
1 teaspoon pure vanilla extract
1 teaspoon grated lemon zest
Unsalted butter
2 ripe bananas, diced, plus extra for serving
Pure maple syrup

In a medium bowl, sift together the flour, sugar, baking powder, and salt. Whisk together the sour cream, milk, eggs, vanilla, and lemon zest. Add the wet ingredients to the dry ones, mixing only until combined.

Melt 1 tablespoon of butter in a large skillet over medium-low heat until it bubbles. Ladle the pancake batter into the pan. Distribute a rounded tablespoon of bananas on each pancake. Cook for 2 to 3 minutes, until bubbles appear on top and the underside is nicely browned. Flip the pancakes and then cook for another minute, until browned. Wipe out the pan with a paper towel, add more butter to the pan, and continue cooking pancakes until all the batter is used. Serve with sliced bananas, butter, and maple syrup.

I use a ¼-cup measure to drop the batter into the pan.

The pancakes will stay warm in a preheated 200-degree oven for 15 to 20 minutes.

SLOW-COOKED SCRAMBLED EGGS
THREE WAYS

It's not so hard to take a family classic and update it so breakfast feels like a special occasion. Here are three versions of scrambled eggs that are easy enough to make any day but delicious enough for a New Year's Day party. It will take about 10 minutes to cook these, but the creamy results are really worth the time.

with Fresh Herbs

Serves 6

16 extra-large eggs
1 ¼ cups half-and-half
2 teaspoons kosher salt
½ teaspoon freshly ground black pepper
4 tablespoons (½ stick) unsalted butter, divided
1 tablespoon finely chopped fresh parsley
1 tablespoon finely chopped scallions, white and green parts
1 tablespoon finely chopped fresh dill

Whisk the eggs in a bowl with the half-and-half, salt, and pepper. Heat 2 tablespoons of butter in a large sauté or omelet pan. Add the eggs and cook them over medium-low heat, stirring constantly, until the desired doneness. Off the heat, add the remaining 2 tablespoons of butter, the parsley, scallions, and dill. Stir until the butter is melted. Check for seasonings. Serve hot.

with Goat Cheese

Serves 6

16 extra-large eggs
1 ¼ cups milk or half-and-half
1 ½ teaspoons kosher salt
¾ teaspoon freshly ground black pepper
4 tablespoons (½ stick) unsalted butter, divided
6 ounces fresh goat cheese, such as Montrachet, crumbled
2 tablespoons minced fresh chives

Whisk the eggs in a bowl with the milk, salt, and pepper. Heat 2 tablespoons of butter in a large sauté or omelet pan. Add the eggs and cook them over medium-low heat, stirring constantly, until the desired doneness. Off the heat, add the goat cheese, chives, and the remaining 2 tablespoons of butter. Stir and allow the eggs to sit for 30 seconds, until the cheese begins to melt. Check for seasonings. Serve hot.

with Caviar

Serves 6

16 extra-large eggs
1 ¼ cups half-and-half
1 ½ teaspoons kosher salt
½ teaspoon freshly ground black pepper
4 tablespoons (½ stick) unsalted butter, divided
125 grams malossol caviar, ossetra or sevruga

Whisk the eggs in a bowl with the half-and-half, salt, and pepper. Heat 2 tablespoons of butter in a large sauté or omelet pan. Add the eggs and cook them over medium-low heat, stirring constantly, until the desired doneness. Off the heat, add the remaining 2 tablespoons of butter and stir until it's melted. Check for seasonings. Serve hot and pass the caviar.

"Malossol" means "without salt" and indicates that the caviar is packed with a minimum of added salt.

POTATO BASIL FRITTATA

Serves 8

The first time I met my dear friend Anna Pump, who owns the amazing specialty food store Loaves and Fishes, she invited me to her house for lunch. She served the first frittata I'd ever had and I'll never forget how delicious it was. This recipe and the next one are inspired by that lunch. They're also an easy breakfast to make for a crowd.

8 tablespoons (1 stick) unsalted butter, divided
2 cups peeled and ½-inch-diced boiling potatoes
   (4 potatoes)
8 extra-large eggs
15 ounces ricotta cheese
¾ pound Gruyère cheese, grated
½ teaspoon kosher salt
½ teaspoon freshly ground black pepper
¾ cup chopped fresh basil leaves
⅓ cup all-purpose flour
¾ teaspoon baking powder

Preheat the oven to 350 degrees.

Melt 3 tablespoons of the butter in a 10-inch oven-proof omelet pan over medium-low heat. Add the potatoes and fry them until cooked through, turning often, 10 to 15 minutes. Melt the remaining 5 tablespoons of butter in a small dish in the microwave.

Meanwhile, whisk the eggs in a large bowl, then stir in the ricotta, Gruyère, melted butter, salt, pepper, and basil. Sprinkle on the flour and baking powder and stir into the egg mixture.

Pour the egg mixture over the potatoes and place the pan in the center of the oven. Bake the frittata until it is browned and puffed, 50 minutes to an hour. It will be rounded and firm in the middle and a knife inserted in the frittata should come out clean. Serve hot.

SMOKED SALMON FRITTATA

Serves 8

1 medium onion, diced
1 tablespoon unsalted butter
12 extra-large eggs
1 cup heavy cream
4 ounces fresh goat cheese, such as Montrachet, crumbled
½ pound smoked salmon, chopped
3 scallions, chopped, white and light green parts
3 tablespoons chopped fresh dill
1 teaspoon kosher salt
½ teaspoon freshly ground black pepper

Preheat the oven to 350 degrees.

Sauté the onion and butter in a 10-inch oven-proof omelet pan over medium-low heat until translucent, about 5 minutes.

In a large bowl, beat the eggs. Add the heavy cream, goat cheese, smoked salmon, scallions, dill, salt, and pepper and combine. Pour the mixture over the onions and place the omelet pan in the center of the oven. Bake the frittata for about 50 minutes, until it puffs and a knife inserted in the middle comes out clean. Serve hot directly from the pan.

CHALLAH FRENCH TOAST

Makes 8 large slices

This is Sunday breakfast with the volume turned up. You can use leftover challah from the freezer, and the orange zest comes from the oranges you're going to squeeze for fresh juice. The rest you probably have around the house. And your family will love you.

6 extra-large eggs
1 ½ cups half-and-half or milk
1 teaspoon grated orange zest
½ teaspoon pure vanilla extract
1 tablespoon good honey
½ teaspoon kosher salt
1 large loaf of challah or brioche bread
Unsalted butter
Vegetable oil

TO SERVE
Pure maple syrup
Good raspberry preserves (optional)
Sifted confectioners' sugar (optional)

Preheat the oven to 250 degrees.

In a large shallow bowl, whisk together the eggs, half-and-half, orange zest, vanilla, honey, and salt. Slice the challah in ¾-inch-thick slices. Soak as many slices in the egg mixture as possible for 5 minutes, turning once.

Heat 1 tablespoon butter and 1 tablespoon oil in a very large sauté pan over medium heat. Add the soaked bread and cook for 2 to 3 minutes on each side, until nicely browned. Place the cooked French toast on a sheet pan and keep it warm in the oven. Fry the remaining soaked bread slices, adding butter and oil as needed, until it's all cooked. Serve hot with maple syrup, raspberry preserves, and/or confectioners' sugar.

HASHED BROWNS

Serves 4 to 6

These are delicious served for breakfast with scrambled eggs (see pages 178–181) and turkey sausages, but when my husband tasted them he wanted to know if he could have them for dinner! Hey, why not? Whatever makes him happy is just fine with me.

> 5 tablespoons unsalted butter
> 1 ½ pounds boiling potatoes, peeled and ½-inch diced
> 1 ½ cups chopped yellow onions (2 onions)
> 2 teaspoons kosher salt
> 1 teaspoon freshly ground black pepper
> 2 tablespoons minced fresh flat-leaf parsley
> 2 tablespoons minced scallions, white and green parts

Melt the butter in a large (10- to 12-inch) sauté pan. Add the potatoes, onions, salt, and pepper and cook over medium-low heat for 15 to 20 minutes, turning occasionally with a flat spatula, until the potatoes are evenly browned and cooked through. (Allow the potatoes to cook for 5 minutes before turning.) Turn off the heat and add the parsley and scallions. Serve hot.

Use any leftover potatoes in Potato Basil Frittata (page 182) for lunch.

You can peel and dice the potatoes early and keep them in the refrigerator in a bowl of cold water. Drain them and dry them well with paper towels before frying.

SCALLION CREAM CHEESE

Serves 6

Some specialty food stores make cream cheese in flavors like chocolate and rum raisin, which offends the purist in me. Barefoot Contessa sells lots of scallion cream cheese, but vegetable cream cheese on a bagel is my favorite. And there's nothing as delicious as homemade. These three stay fresh for days in the refrigerator.

16 ounces cream cheese, at room temperature
½ cup chopped scallions, white and green parts
   (4 scallions)
2 tablespoons milk
¼ teaspoon kosher salt

Place the cream cheese, scallions, milk, and salt in the bowl of a food processor fitted with the steel blade and process until smooth.

GARLIC & HERB CREAM CHEESE

Serves 6

16 ounces cream cheese, at room temperature
2 tablespoons minced scallions, white and green parts
2 tablespoons minced fresh dill
2 tablespoons minced fresh parsley
2 teaspoons minced garlic
2 tablespoons milk
¼ teaspoon kosher salt

Place the cream cheese, scallions, dill, parsley, garlic, milk, and salt in the bowl of an elecric mixer fitted with the paddle attachment and mix on low speed until blended.

VEGETABLE CREAM CHEESE

Serves 6

16 ounces cream cheese, at room temperature
2 tablespoons minced scallions, white and green parts
2 tablespoons finely chopped carrot
2 tablespoons finely chopped celery
2 tablespoons finely chopped radish (2 radishes)
2 to 3 pinches kosher salt
1 pinch finely ground black pepper

Place the cream cheese, scallions, carrot, celery, radish, salt, and pepper in the bowl of an electric mixer fitted with the paddle attachment and mix on low speed until blended.

CHIVE BISCUITS

Makes 8 biscuits

These biscuits have the flavor of old-fashioned baking-powder biscuits and the lightness of the scones at Barefoot Contessa. They're also delicious baked on top of my chicken stew (page 90).

> 2 cups all-purpose flour
> 1 tablespoon baking powder
> 1 teaspoon kosher salt
> 1 teaspoon sugar
> ¼ pound (1 stick) cold unsalted butter, diced
> ¾ cup half-and-half
> ½ cup chopped fresh chives or fresh parsley
> 1 egg mixed with 1 tablespoon water, for egg wash

Preheat the oven to 400 degrees.

Combine the flour, baking powder, salt, and sugar in the bowl of an electric mixer fitted with the paddle attachment. Add the butter and mix on low speed until the butter is the size of peas. With the mixer on low, add the half-and-half and beat until just mixed. Add the chives and mix until just combined.

Dump the dough out on a well-floured board and knead lightly into a rectangle ¾ inch thick. Cut out rounds with a 2½-inch round cutter and place on a sheet pan lined with parchment paper. Brush with the egg wash.

Bake for 20 to 22 minutes, until the tops are browned and the insides are firm. Serve warm.

FRESH FRUIT WITH HONEY VANILLA YOGURT

Serves 4 to 6

Here's a simple way to make fresh fruit a treat for breakfast. It's so easy to stir together and it lasts for a week in the refrigerator.

2 cups plain yogurt
2 tablespoons good honey
½ teaspoon pure vanilla extract
Seeds scraped from ½ vanilla bean (optional)
½ pint fresh blueberries
½ pint fresh raspberries
1 pint fresh strawberries, hulled and cut in half
1 papaya, peeled, seeded, and diced

Combine the yogurt, honey, vanilla extract, and vanilla bean seeds, if using. Gently mix the berries and papaya together. Spoon the fruit into serving bowls and top with the yogurt.

I use Dannon regular yogurt or Stonyfield Farm low-fat.

KIDS!

PARMESAN Chicken Sticks

Mac & CHEESE

BROCCOLI & Bow Ties

Fruit Juice SHAPES

JAM Thumbprint Cookies

WHIPPED Hot Chocolate

HOMEMADE Marshmallows

Toasted Coconut MARSHMALLOWS

BIRTHDAY Sheet Cake

Entertaining Kids

Years ago, my friend Marilyn Bethany asked her twelve-year-old daughter, Maisie, how she wanted to celebrate her birthday. Maisie said she wanted to have a cocktail party! A cocktail party? Marilyn thought it was such a funny idea that she decided to do it. Her husband, Ed Tivnan, dressed in a tuxedo as the bartender and served "strawberry daiquiris" (without the rum, of course!) in champagne flutes. Marilyn and I wore black skirts, white shirts, and black bow ties like waiters and served "hors d'oeuvres" (Chinese takeout on silver catering trays). The girls all spent the afternoon playing grown-up and putting on airs with one another. As I leaned down to one of the girls to offer a spare rib, I asked, "Excuse me, madam, would you like a spare rib?" She tasted one. "Delicious," she said, "send my compliments to the chef!" Marilyn and I never laughed so hard in our lives.

Entertaining kids can be a challenge, but you don't have to resort to pin-the-tail-on-the donkey. Kids love to play grown-up for the day and you can draw on your own life experience. My friend Joanne Shumski, who owns a beauty salon, invites all her daughter's friends for an afternoon of "beauty," which is basically a little nail polish, some lip gloss, a few curlers, and take-out pizza. I like to invite children for a cooking class: we make macaroni and cheese and a salad and decorate the birthday cake, which, of course, then becomes lunch. We all have a great time, the kids learn to cook, and all I have to do is shop and bake the cake.

When I'm speaking to groups around the country, I am often asked for ideas on entertaining kids. I remember one woman who had a terrific idea. She invites her friends for a dinner party, as usual, but asks them to bring their children. In another room, she makes a separate dinner party for the kids only and hires a baby-sitter or two to preside. The parents don't feel guilty that they've left the kids at home, and the kids have a great time together. Everybody wins.

PARMESAN CHICKEN STICKS

Makes 14 to 16 sticks

If you're having a party for grown-ups and want to make a party for the kids at the same time, why not prepare Parmesan Chicken (page 82) for your friends and the same chicken on sticks for the kids? They're so much fun to eat that you'll have to keep the grown-ups away from the kids' table. Use ice-cream sticks for small children so they don't hurt themselves on the skewers.

1 ½ pounds skinless, boneless chicken breasts (3 to 4)
1 cup all-purpose flour
1 teaspoon kosher salt
½ teaspoon freshly ground black pepper
2 extra-large eggs
1 cup seasoned bread crumbs
½ cup grated Parmesan cheese
Unsalted butter
Good olive oil
Bamboo skewers (6 to 10 inches long) or ice-cream sticks

Lay the chicken breasts on a cutting board and slice each diagonally into four or five large strips.

Combine the flour, salt, and pepper on a dinner plate. Beat the eggs with 1 tablespoon of water on a second plate. Combine the bread crumbs and Parmesan cheese on a third plate. Dredge the chicken breasts on both sides in the flour mixture, then dip both sides into the egg mixture and roll in the bread-crumb mixture, pressing lightly to coat.

Heat 1 tablespoon of butter and 1 tablespoon of olive oil in a large sauté pan and cook the chicken strips on medium-low heat for about 3 minutes on each side, until just cooked through. Don't crowd the pan. Add more butter and oil and cook the rest of the chicken breasts. Serve each strip on a skewer or stick.

You can keep the chicken breasts warm for about 15 minutes on a sheet pan in a 200-degree oven.

MAC & CHEESE

Serves 6 to 8

I know that mac & cheese is considered kids' food, but the tomatoes and bread crumbs on top of this one make it fit for company. And it's still the feel-good food you want to eat. Perfect!

Kosher salt
Vegetable oil
1 pound elbow macaroni or cavatappi (see Note)
1 quart milk
8 tablespoons (1 stick) unsalted butter, divided
½ cup all-purpose flour
12 ounces Gruyère cheese, grated (4 cups)
8 ounces extra-sharp Cheddar, grated (2 cups)
½ teaspoon freshly ground black pepper
½ teaspoon nutmeg
¾ pound fresh tomatoes (4 small)
1½ cups fresh white bread crumbs (5 slices, crusts removed)

Preheat the oven to 375 degrees.

Drizzle oil into a large pot of boiling salted water. Add the macaroni and cook according to the directions on the package, 6 to 8 minutes. Drain well.

Meanwhile, heat the milk in a small saucepan, but don't boil it. Melt 6 tablespoons of butter in a large (4-quart) pot and add the flour. Cook over low heat for 2 minutes, stirring with a whisk. While whisking, add the hot milk and cook for a minute or two more, until thickened and smooth. Off the heat, add the Gruyère, Cheddar, 1 tablespoon salt, pepper, and nutmeg. Add the cooked macaroni and stir well. Pour into a 3-quart baking dish.

Slice the tomatoes and arrange on top. Melt the remaining 2 tablespoons of butter, combine them with the fresh bread crumbs, and sprinkle on the top. Bake for 30 to 35 minutes, or until the sauce is bubbly and the macaroni is browned on the top.

Instead of elbow macaroni, it's fun to use cavatappi, a corkscrew-shaped pasta by De Cecco, if you can find it.

To make ahead, put the macaroni and cheese in the baking dish, cover, and refrigerate until ready to bake. Put the tomatoes and bread crumbs on top and bake for about 40 to 50 minutes.

BROCCOLI & BOW TIES

Serves 6 to 8

This is easy to make and the kids will even eat the broccoli if it's served with bow ties. If I'm making another pasta for dinner, I sometimes serve the broccoli without the bow ties and it's delicious.

> Kosher salt
> 8 cups broccoli florets (4 heads)
> ½ pound farfalle (bow tie) pasta
> 2 tablespoons unsalted butter
> 2 tablespoons good olive oil
> 1 teaspoon minced garlic
> Zest of 1 lemon
> ½ teaspoon freshly ground black pepper
> 1 tablespoon freshly squeezed lemon juice
> ¼ cup toasted pignoli (pine) nuts
> Freshly grated Parmesan cheese, optional

Cook the broccoli for 3 minutes in a large pot of boiling salted water. Remove the broccoli from the water with a slotted spoon or sieve. Place in a large bowl and set aside.

In the same water, cook the bow-tie pasta according to the package directions, about 12 minutes. Drain well and add to the broccoli.

Meanwhile, in a small sauté pan, heat the butter and oil and cook the garlic and lemon zest over medium-low heat for 1 minute. Off the heat, add 2 teaspoons salt, the pepper, and lemon juice and pour this over the broccoli and pasta. Toss well. Season to taste, sprinkle with the pignolis and cheese, if using, and serve.

To toast pignolis, place them in a dry sauté pan over medium-low heat and cook, tossing often, for about 5 minutes, until light brown.

This can be made in advance and reheated in the microwave.

FRUIT JUICE SHAPES

Makes 20 pieces

Kids love finger foods when they're cut into fun shapes. I wanted to make these with ingredients that are good for them and taste delicious. So I used all kinds of fruit juice and they're terrific. And it's just as easy as making Jell-O!

4 cups pure grape juice, pure white grape juice,
   cranberry juice cocktail, or other clear juice
4 envelopes unflavored gelatin

In a large bowl, sprinkle the gelatin over 1 cup of the juice and allow to stand for a few minutes. Meanwhile, heat the remaining 3 cups of juice until just boiling and pour it over the juice and gelatin mixture. Stir until the gelatin is dissolved.

Pour into a 9 × 9-inch pan and chill until firm, about 3 hours or overnight. Dip the pan briefly into hot water to loosen, cut into squares or shapes, and serve.

You can make this with juices that aren't clear, such as orange juice, but they don't have that shimmery, translucent quality. But if you want your kids to "eat" their orange juice, why not?

JAM THUMBPRINT COOKIES

Makes 32 cookies

Here is yet another variation of my friend Eli Zabar's wonderful shortbread. I make one recipe of shortbread dough and then make lots of different cookies with it, such as shortbread hearts, linzer cookies (The Barefoot Contessa Cookbook), and these jam thumbprints. Your family will think you've baked all day, but your secret's safe with me.

¾ pound (3 sticks) unsalted butter, at room temperature
1 cup sugar
1 teaspoon pure vanilla extract
3½ cups all-purpose flour
¼ teaspoon kosher salt
1 egg beaten with 1 tablespoon water, for egg wash
7 ounces sweetened flaked coconut
Raspberry and/or apricot jam

Preheat the oven to 350 degrees.

In an electric mixer fitted with the paddle attachment, cream together the butter and sugar until they are just combined and then add the vanilla. Separately, sift together the flour and salt. With the mixer on low speed, add the flour mixture to the creamed butter and sugar. Mix until the dough starts to come together. Dump on a floured board and roll together into a flat disc. Wrap in plastic wrap and chill for 30 minutes.

Roll the dough into 1¼-inch balls. (If you have a scale, they should each weigh 1 ounce.) Dip each ball into the egg wash and then roll it in coconut. Place the balls on an ungreased cookie sheet and press a light indentation into the top of each with your finger. Drop ¼ teaspoon of jam into each indentation. Bake for 20 to 25 minutes, until the coconut is a golden brown. Cool and serve.

WHIPPED HOT CHOCOLATE

Serves 4 to 5

This originally appeared in The Barefoot Contessa Cookbook *and I'm only repeating it because I found out that it's so much better whipped. It gets a froth on the top like a cappuccino, which for some reason makes the whole thing taste better. I tried whipping it in my blender, which unfortunately doesn't have a tight seal, and I ended up wearing most of the first batch. If you have a hand-held immersion blender, it's really the best option.*

> 2 ½ cups whole milk
> 2 cups half-and-half
> 4 ounces semisweet chocolate chips
> 4 ounces milk chocolate, chopped
> 1 tablespoon sugar
> 1 teaspoon pure vanilla extract
> 1 teaspoon decaffeinated instant coffee powder
> Homemade Marshmallows (recipe follows), optional

Heat the milk and half-and-half in a large saucepan over medium heat to just below the simmering point. Remove the pan from the heat and add both chocolates. When the chocolates are melted, stir in the sugar, vanilla, and coffee powder. Reheat gently.

To froth the hot chocolate, whip it in the saucepan with an immersion blender. If you're very careful, you can also pour it into the jar of a blender with a tight seal and blend on high speed for about 30 seconds. Pour into cups and serve as is or with homemade marshmallows.

HOMEMADE MARSHMALLOWS

Makes 20 to 40 marshmallows

Forget those rubbery, flavorless things you buy at the grocery store. These marshmallows are light and flavorful, and they melt in your mouth. The kids love to make them (be sure an adult makes the syrup!) and they can put them in everything from hot chocolate to s'mores. Or, just pop these vanilla pillows into your mouth for a little pick-me-up.

3 packages unflavored gelatin
1 ½ cups granulated sugar
1 cup light corn syrup
¼ teaspoon kosher salt
1 tablespoon pure vanilla extract
Confectioners' sugar, for dusting

Combine the gelatin and ½ cup of cold water in the bowl of an electric mixer fitted with the whisk attachment and allow to sit while you make the syrup.

Meanwhile, combine the sugar, corn syrup, salt, and ½ cup water in a small saucepan and cook over medium heat until the sugar dissolves. Raise the heat to high and cook until the syrup reaches 240 degrees on a candy thermometer. Remove from the heat.

With the mixer on low speed, slowly pour the sugar syrup into the dissolved gelatin. Put the mixer on high speed and whip until the mixture is very thick, about 15 minutes. Add the vanilla and mix thoroughly.

With a sieve, generously dust an 8 × 12-inch nonmetal baking dish with confectioners' sugar. Pour the marshmallow mixture into the pan, smooth the top, and dust with more confectioners' sugar. Allow to stand uncovered overnight until it dries out.

Turn the marshmallows onto a board and cut them in squares. Dust them with more confectioners' sugar.

TOASTED COCONUT
MARSHMALLOWS

Makes 20 to 40 marshmallows

You can add lots of flavorings to the outside of marshmallows. My favorite is toasted coconut, but you can dip them in chocolate, roll them in cinnamon sugar, or just eat them plain. They're all delicious and the kids will love thinking up their own combinations.

7 ounces sweetened shredded coconut, toasted
1 recipe Homemade Marshmallow batter (page 211)
Confectioners' sugar

Sprinkle half the toasted coconut in an 8 × 12-inch nonmetal pan. Pour in the marshmallow batter and smooth the top of the mixture with damp hands. Sprinkle on the remaining toasted coconut. Allow to dry uncovered at room temperature overnight.

Remove the marshmallows from the pan and cut into squares. Roll the sides of each piece carefully in confectioners' sugar. Store uncovered at room temperature.

To toast coconut, place it in a very large dry sauté pan and cook, over low heat, for 15 to 20 minutes, tossing frequently, until lightly browned.

BIRTHDAY SHEET CAKE

Makes one 12 × 18-inch cake

My friend Taylor Lupica made a cake like this for her daughter Hannah and niece Maggie for their birthdays and they had a ball decorating it with M&M's. I thought it was such a good idea that I came up with my own version. I've found that white cake and chocolate frosting is almost every kid's favorite combination. This makes a very generous amount of frosting, so little fingers can clean the bowl.

FOR THE CAKE
18 tablespoons (2¼ sticks) unsalted butter, at room temperature
3 cups sugar
6 extra-large eggs, at room temperature
8 ounces (about 1 cup) sour cream, at room temperature
1½ teaspoons pure vanilla extract
Zest of 1 lemon
3 cups all-purpose flour
⅓ cup cornstarch
1 teaspoon kosher salt
1 teaspoon baking soda

FOR THE FROSTING
24 ounces semisweet chocolate chips
1½ cups heavy cream
2 tablespoons light corn syrup
½ teaspoon pure vanilla extract
4 tablespoons (½ stick) unsalted butter, at room temperature

M&M's candy for decorating

Preheat the oven to 350 degrees. Butter and flour a 12 × 18 × 1½-inch sheet pan.

To make the cake, cream the butter and sugar on medium-high speed in the bowl of an electric mixer fitted with a paddle attachment until light and fluffy, about 5 minutes. On medium speed, add the eggs, two at a time, then the sour cream, vanilla, and lemon zest, scraping down the bowl as needed.

Mix well. Sift together the flour, cornstarch, salt, and baking soda. With the mixer on low speed, slowly add the flour mixture to the butter mixture and stir just until smooth. Finish mixing by hand to be sure the batter is well mixed. Pour evenly into the pan, smooth the top with a spatula, and bake in the center of the oven for 25 to 30 minutes, or until a toothpick comes out clean. Cool in the pan to room temperature.

For the frosting, place the chocolate chips and heavy cream in a bowl set over a pot of simmering water, stirring occasionally, until the chips are completely melted. Off the heat, add the corn syrup and vanilla and allow the chocolate mixture to cool to room temperature. In the bowl of an electric mixer fitted with the whisk attachment, whisk the chocolate mixture and softened butter on medium speed for a few minutes, until it's thickened.

Spread the frosting evenly on the cake. Have the children decorate the cake with M&M's.

I often serve this right in the pan. If you want to turn the cake out onto a serving platter or board, line the baking pan with parchment after you butter it, then butter and flour the paper.

NINE INGREDIENTS
you'll use over and over

I don't think you need a shelf full of esoteric ingredients to make delicious food. Almost everything in my recipes can be made with foods from your local grocery store, plus maybe a few extra pantry items from a specialty food store or wine shop. After all, why write recipes that are easy to make if it takes all day to shop for wild mushrooms and Meyer lemons? Personally, I'd rather cook than shop! Many people have asked me for my favorite ingredients, so here they are:

De Cecco dry pastas

Kosher salt

Olio Santo extra-virgin olive oil

Hellmann's mayonnaise

Tellicherry black peppercorns

Aged Italian Parmesan cheese (Parmigiano-Reggiano)

Nielsen-Massey pure vanilla extract

Heckers unbleached all-purpose flour

Grey Poupon Dijon mustard

TEN KITCHEN TOOLS
you'll use over and over

I have a pet peeve about kitchen equipment: I hate to find a recipe that I want to make and then realize it requires a piece of equipment that I don't own and I know I'll never use again. I also hate kitchen equipment that has only one use. We've all been seduced by that fancy garlic press, then realized that a knife just does a better job. As a professional cook, I have a pretty well-equipped kitchen at home, but I find I tend to use the same few items over and over again. Why have loaf pans in six different sizes when one size will do? Some of the items listed below, such as a KitchenAid mixer, are expensive but are so worth the investment because they last a lifetime. Others, while inexpensive, are truly indispensable. These are ten things I use on a regular basis. I think that they will really give you the pleasure of knowing you have the right tool for the job.

Braun electric juicer

Stainless-steel mixing bowls from 2 quarts to 8 quarts

Cuisinart food processor

Parchment paper

12 x 18 x 1½-inch stainless-steel sheet pans

Good-quality knives; one paring, one 8-inch chef's, one serrated blade

Rasp zester

KitchenAid electric mixer

Oven thermometer

10- and 12-inch All-Clad sauté pans

2 LB HEALTH LOAF

Ingredients- Stone Ground Whole Wheat Flour,
Water, Natural Sour, Sunflower seeds, Sesame
Seeds, Flax seeds, Honey, Yeast And Salt

MENUS

Breakfast

BREAKFAST WITH THE KIDS
Fresh orange juice
Banana Sour Cream Pancakes *with maple syrup*
Crispy bacon
Coffee

WINTER BREAKFAST
Fresh orange juice
Soft Scrambled Eggs with Fresh Herbs
Chive Biscuits
Honeydew melon and blueberries
Whipped Hot Chocolate

SUNDAY BREAKFAST
Challah French Toast *with butter and maple syrup*
Turkey sausages
Sliced oranges
Coffee

NEW YEAR'S BREAKFAST
Champagne and blood orange juice
Soft Scrambled Eggs with Caviar
Blueberry Coffee Cake Muffins
Long-stemmed strawberries
Coffee

SUMMER BRUNCH
Bloody Marys
Smoked Salmon Frittata
Hashed Browns
Toasted Bagels with Vegetable Cream Cheese
Fresh Fruit with Honey Vanilla Yogurt

Lunch

WINTER LUNCH
  East Hampton Clam Chowder
  Green Salad with Creamy Mustard Vinaigrette
  French bread
  Apples, English Cheddar, and Coconut Macaroons

SPRING LUNCH
  Penne with Five Cheeses
  Garlic Sautéed Spinach
  Italian bread
  Stewed Berries & Ice Cream

SUMMER LUNCH
  Tuna Tartare
  Lobster Cobb Salad
  French bread
  Summer Pudding with Rum Whipped Cream

SUMMER PICNIC
  Chicken with Tabbouleh *(without tomatoes)*
  Cherry tomatoes with chopped basil
  Sourdough bread
  Orange Pound Cake
  Fresh peaches

SUMMER SALADS FOR LUNCH
  Montauk Seafood Salad
  Sliced Tomato, Mozzarella, and Basil
  Whole-grain bread
  Lemon Angel Food Cake
  Fresh raspberries

Dinner

WINTER DINNER
Oven-Fried Chicken
Mashed Potatoes & Gravy
Sautéed Carrots
String Beans with Shallots
Deep-Dish Apple Pie

LAST-MINUTE SUMMER SUPPER
Arugula with Parmesan
Linguine with Shrimp Scampi
French bread
Stewed Berries & Ice Cream

FAMILY DINNER
Chicken Stew with Biscuits
Green Salad with Creamy Mustard Vinaigrette
Plain Cheesecake *and fresh raspberries*

FOURTH OF JULY DINNER
Tuna Tartare
Tequila Lime Chicken
Sagaponack Corn Pudding
Sliced tomatoes
Flag Cake

SUNDAY FAMILY DINNER
Sunday Rib Roast with Mustard Horseradish Sauce
String Beans with Shallots
Mashed Butternut Squash
Rum Raisin Rice Pudding

ITALIAN NIGHT
Arugula with Parmesan
Real Meatballs and Spaghetti
Garlic bread
Tiramisù

WINTER DINNER PARTY
Warm roasted cashews
Endive, Stilton & Walnuts
Saffron Risotto with Butternut Squash
Espresso Ice Cream *with biscotti from a bakery*

MAKE-AHEAD WINTER DINNER
Roasted Winter Vegetable Soup
Brioche Croutons
Penne with Five Cheeses
Green Salad with Creamy Mustard Vinaigrette
Bosc pears, English Stilton, and a glass of port

SATURDAY DINNER WITH COMPANY
Endive, Stilton & walnuts
Herb Roasted Lamb *(with potatoes)*
String Beans with Shallots
Pumpkin Banana Mousse Tart

DINNER WITH KIDS
Mac & Cheese
Broccoli & Bow Ties *(without the bow ties)*
French bread
Frozen Key Lime Pie

CHILDREN'S BIRTHDAY PARTY
Buffalo Chicken Wings
Fruit Juice Shapes
Parmesan Chicken Sticks
Broccoli & Bow Ties
Birthday Sheet Cake

If you have other Barefoot Contessa cookbooks and would like to receive an extended list of menus using recipes from all the books, please e-mail me at Ina@BarefootContessa.com.

CREDITS

Unless otherwise indicated, tableware shown in the photographs is privately owned. All the antique wire racks are from the collection of Sue Richmond.

page 31: bowl from Lucca (631-329-8298)
page 32: bowl from Inside Out (631-329-3600)
page 38: plate from Tabletop Designs by Stephanie Queller (631-283-1313)
page 58: plate from Crate and Barrel (800-967-6696)
page 68: itcher from Crate and Barrel
page 125: bowl from Barney's (212-826-8900)
page 126: plate from Crate and Barrel
page 134: fork from Tabletop Designs
page 140: glass from Tabletop Designs
page 150: plate from Tabletop Designs
page 165: plate from Calvin Klein (212-292-9000)
        fabric from Sage Street Antiques (631-725-4036)
page 176: plate from Barney's
page 179: fork from Tabletop Designs
page 204: plate from Crate and Barrel
page 228: bowl from Lucca

INDEX

RECIPE INDEX